# THE VERY BEST FROM

*Hallmark*

## GREETING CARDS
## THROUGH THE YEARS

# THE VERY BEST FROM

## *Hallmark*

### GREETING CARDS
### THROUGH THE YEARS

*Ellen Stern*

HARRY N. ABRAMS, INC., PUBLISHERS, NEW YORK

*For Peter, Charley,*
*Kate, and Herman,*
*my nearest and dearest*

Project Coordinator: Naomi Warner
Editor: Eric Himmel
Designer: Raymond P. Hooper
Photographer: Michael J. Pastor, Hallmark


Library of Congress Cataloging-in-Publication Data

Stern, Ellen Stock.
The very best from Hallmark: greeting cards through the years/
Ellen Stern.
p.     cm.
ISBN 0-8109-1745-9
1. Greeting cards—United States—Catalogs. 2. Hallmark Cards,
Inc.—Catalogs. I. Hallmark Cards, Inc. II. Title.
NC 1864.H3S74 1988
741.68'4'0977841—dc19                               88-3298
                                                     CIP

Published in 1988 by Harry N. Abrams, Incorporated, New York

A Times Mirror Company

Printed and bound in Japan

# Contents

*'S wonderful! 'S marvelous!—*
*You should care for me!*
　　　　　—Ira Gershwin

# *Introduction*

'S true. It's what greeting cards are all about. It's why people spend $3.9 billion to buy seven billion of them a year — and why Hallmark, the world's largest producer, turns out eleven million of them every day.

The greeting card serves us right. It is greeting and card and keepsake and tonic, trophy and legacy, passion and praise. It shows that we care.

We will probably never know the name of the well-

*Joyce C. Hall in an early*
*Kansas City portrait*

meaning person who invented it. But he or she was, as is so often the case, undoubtedly an Egyptian. History tells us that the first card-worthy occasion was the New Year and that when a gift was delivered from one sunbaked-brick bungalow to another, a message went with it. In such a manner—written on papyrus or uttered by the messenger—were the world's first greetings bestowed.

The Romans followed with copper pennies showing their two-faced god, Janus, then with pictured greetings on terra cotta and on medals. The next known example, a woodcut commemorating the New Year, appeared somewhere in Germany in 1450. But no card would take off until 1840, when Parliament passed the Postage Act in England, making it possible to send mail for a penny. In the United States today, greeting cards come from some eight hundred makers and comprise 50 percent of the first-class mail— and more are published by Hallmark than anyone else.

The new era dawned with Joyce Clyde Hall, born in 1891—in the month of August, which is, truth to tell, the number one ranking birthday month. This son of Nebraska was an all-American boy. Lincolnlike, he walked miles to school in every season. He also dipped girls' braids in the inkwell, heard William Jennings Bryan orate, acquired a puppy he named Teddy after the president, dispensed handbills on prohibition, read Zane Grey and *American Magazine*, sold lemonade at the ball park, carried water at the circus, and risked life and limb celebrating the Fourth of July with a boodle of firecrackers. And all the while he dreamed one dream: "If I ever made any money," he would write in his 1979 autobiography, "every day I would have a baked potato with three pieces of butter." (The dream probably came true. In 1935, Hall would buy himself a herd of Jerseys and have himself a farm, bringing in squash and sweet corn to sell to employees in the Hallmark parking lot. "If I had it to do over again," he liked to say, meaning not a word of it, "I'd open a restaurant.")

At the turn of the century in small-town America, the local bookstore was also the source of magazines, newspapers, cigars, and candy, especially hand-dipped chocolates. It was just so with the Hall family's store in Norfolk,

Nebraska. But things were soon to change. It happened one night that a traveling salesman stopped by with his case of picture postcards. Young Joyce Hall, his captive audience, was captivated.

After a rapid number of entrees into the world of retailing (the boy sold, at various stages of his youth, horseradish, popcorn, lilac cologne, and tooth powder), he was ready to take on and wholesale these colorful communiqués decorated with lush landscapes, rosy-cheeked moppets, sprigs of holly, doves bearing voluminous bouquets. They bore birthday greetings, waggish wisecracks, Christmas cheer, touristy tidings from Woonsocket and Luna Park. More for the pictures than for the messages they carried from Cousin Edna, they were cherished and then collected in bulky albums. The works Hall saw were probably German imports: when the postcard craze hit in 1903, upstaging fussy greeting cards of the Victorian era, German lithography—good and bad—dominated the market.

Hall persuaded his two older brothers to join him in what he had already named the Norfolk Post Card Company. With brother Rollie as chief salesman, working the territories, and brother Bill as president, sending out the invoices, Joyce was the one to fill the orders. At the age of sixteen he was already the family's moving force. Such gumption came not from his father, certainly—he was an itinerant preacher who managed a hardware store and also managed to patent a wire fly swatter before abandoning his family—but from his grandfathers (who had fought on opposite sides in the Civil War) and from his mother, a woman of fragile health and great pluck.

On January 10, 1910, the Norfolk card game lost its most important player when Joyce Hall emigrated to Kansas City; his brothers would come later. Convinced of "the Kansas City spirit" by a traveling cigar salesman, he was equally convinced of the city's value as a wholesaling and distributing center, thanks to its vast array of railroads and track. His conviction would never change.

Within days, the eighteen-year-old entrepreneur was operating his mail-order postcard business from a twelve-by-twelve top-floor room at the YMCA. He had registered at Spalding's Commercial College to study commercial law, penmanship, spelling, and typing. And he had absorbed Mr. Spalding's credo: "Time is money—save time." Later he would adapt it to "Time is everything—save time," and live with it, and teach his employees to live with it, one legendary example being the egg-timer he liked to place next to the phone.

Postcards were at their peak. As America's passion flowered, as mailbags grew heavier and scrapbooks grew fatter, thousands of printers here and abroad joined the race. In the United States, Detroit Publishing offered some 60,000 different cards—sassy as well as sentimental—at one time. Over there, one of the most prolific was Raphael Tuck & Sons in England. But in Kansas City, there was a fellow who was beginning to lose his conviction. For all the hoo-ha, young Hall felt that, "Postcards were not really a means of communication between people. Most of them were either humorous or simply decorative and lacked a from-me-to-you sentiment; they were sent because it was the thing to do." He observed that, "Personal communication was practically limited to writing letters. But as the pace of life was picking up, people had less time to write long thoughtful letters. Telephones were relatively new, and calling long distance was almost unheard of." What was more, you couldn't *save* a telephone call.

While he contemplated the progress of communication, Hall made progress of his own. Curious, excited, keen to taste it all, he began the business of acquiring savvy. In the bright lights of the big city, he discovered the footlights. There were three legitimate theaters in town, and he attended them regularly, having befriended the local drama critic, a fellow Nebraskan. He also traveled to New York, to the bigger city with the brighter lights, where he visited Grant's Tomb, ate his first raw oysters, and discovered Fifth Avenue.

It was the first of many trips he would take for research. On a trip to New York in the 1940s, accompanied by Hallmark's head of corporate design and a couple of artists, he would visit Lord & Taylor, Bloomingdale's, and Bonwit

Teller—and there be ushered out because the group was taking too many notes on colors, styles, and window displays. Everywhere he roamed he analyzed, assessed, and appreciated the wares and the wonders: at Neiman-Marcus, Bullock's, Gump's, Robinson's, at candy stores and specialty shops.

By 1912, even while the Hall brothers were publishing their own cards of such Kansas City sites as the New Municipal Auditorium, New Union Station, Scene in Electric Park, and Fountain at 9th and Paseo, Joyce Hall was more and more convinced that their time was limited, that greeting cards were due for a renaissance. They represented class, they promised discretion, and, to Hall, they "were more than a form of communication—they were a social custom. While the carriage trade had never taken postcards very seriously, they would buy greeting cards of the finest quality." Indeed, they still do.

The Halls offered valentines as well as greetings for birthdays and Christmas. But in 1915, they lost their hearts when their entire stock of early valentines perished in a January fire. Undaunted, as usual, they pressed on, starting again from scratch and surfacing with a laugh:

*Not little like this tiny pup,*
*But big, just like a dog grown up.*
*I'm wishing you a Merry Christmas.*

It was a beginning.

With the onset of World War I, postcards stopped being imported from Europe, and the market suddenly belonged to America. But domestic quality suffered in comparison, and postcards gave way—as Joyce Hall knew they would— to greeting cards. Anxious mothers and lonely wives could bolster their soldiers' morale with effusive thoughts from home. Joyce Hall was on his way.

Ever the entrepreneur, Joyce Hall knew that he needed more to celebrate than holidays. And so, in 1919, friendship cards entered the line. Shortly afterward, a gentleman entered the office with a poem about friendship he claimed to have

written. Hall liked it, accepted it, engraved it on a card with hand-painted poinsettias for Christmas, saw it become a best-seller, then adapted it for other occasions. But alas! In 1921 there came a gentleman publisher, who announced that the Halls had no right whatever to use the poem, since it had already been published in a book. The publisher demanded that the cards and plates be destroyed and threatened to sue for damages. To ease the situation, Joyce Hall offered the outrageous sum of $500, in cash. Sold. As he remembered it: "Almost everyone felt that we'd never make our money back on this investment, but the poem was so right for greeting cards that I couldn't give it up. It turned out to be one of the best investments we ever made, and 'A Friend's Greeting'—or 'My Friend,' as it's often called— continued to be a best-seller on cards for many years."

The poet was Edgar Guest. The poem is still used on

*A 1928 Hallmark advertisement, using Edgar Guest's poem "My Friend"*

Hallmark cards. Friendship sells. (Although Friendship Day never did. J. C. Hall originated it in 1919, but it didn't take. Says one long-time Hallmark man: "A greeting-card maker can't start a holiday.")

"My Friend" is but one of Hallmark's evergreens, sentiments and situations that are perennially popular and useful on any number of occasions. Elsewhere in the forest: the versatile verse that states "I may not be in Who's Who, but I know what's what"; the get-well card showing an old car going in for repairs; and the 1929 entry announcing "I'd like to Be-Witch-Ya on Halloween." Whimsical compendiums can be illustrated in a variety of styles. One for Mother's Day begins, "Little bluebirds have a mom to feed 'em worms and bugs—Little bunnies have a mom to give them bunny hugs," and proceeds through a veritable menagerie. The pick of the bunch: a four-by-five-inch friendship card featuring a cart of purple pansies that was introduced in February, 1941, for a nickel. Over 25 million have been sold since...and they're still selling, at a rate of about 780,000 a year.

But there is no evergreen more beloved than the Christmas tree. No matter that its popularity comes and goes; so does that of Santa Claus, the poinsettia, the candle, and the bell. Christmas will endure, and so will they. Today's roaring success is, amazingly, the interior fireplace scene—photographed, not painted or drawn. Why? According to Wayne Wormsley, a Hallmark senior planner, "Christmas is, for most people, a traditional season—hearth and home, fond memories—or at least they *think* this is the way things should be."

Other folks go for exteriors, especially U.S. presidents; Hallmark has created greetings for each president since Ike and Mamie popularized mass Yuletide mailings from 1600 Pennsylvania Avenue. In 1969, President and Mrs. Nixon sent out an embossed south view of the White House. In 1974, the Fords sent a lithograph of "The President's House, Washington." The Carters ordered an ink-and-wash drawing of the south view in 1977, and not until the Reagans came in did Christmas come inside again in 1986 with Thomas William Jones's "The East Room at Christmas." The Eisenhowers, Kennedys, and Johnsons asked Hallmark to use the Presidential seal, which knows no season.

No matter how many thousands are sent out by the First Family, no matter how many thousands they are sent, the average American household receives twenty-six cards every Christmas. It is, in the greeting-card world, the number-one holiday. Hallmark has 2,500 different Christmas offerings...and produces them every day of the year.

Valentine's Day is the second largest card-sending holiday after Christmas, and about 850 million are sent every year. Most are given to relatives, but many are not: When else is the teacher so overwhelmingly remembered? It's no surprise that hearts and flowers prevail; that red, white, and pink predominate; but somewhat of a surprise to learn that the tougher the customer, the more lace and frills, the more ornamented a production he wants. The reason is open to speculation, but it may have to do with guilt. The bruiser who's brusque the rest of the year wants passionately to come through now. Somehow, for him (and, one assumes, for his lady) love on a card conquers all.

Distributing and selling the cards is as challenging as making them. In 1914, the Hall Brothers established their first card shop in Kansas City's Corn Belt Bank Building. More important than the stock, which was a little of this, a little of that, was Joyce Hall's knack at inventory control. By rating the cards according to how well they sold, he could—based, at first, on his memory and later on written records—speedily replace those that didn't. It was a system that would evolve into one of the most sophisticated methods in retailing.

There has always been a Hallmark card shop or two in Kansas City. Elsewhere in today's United States, Hallmark owns about 180 shops of the 11,000 going, "but only," says a Hallmark man, "until Mr. or Mrs.—but probably Mrs.—Right comes along."

Most Hallmark stores are independently owned, but the home office keeps in touch. When, for example, the corner pizza parlor begins to fail, in a town that may have Hallmark cards scattered in various stores but no leadership store, Hallmark comes along, works with the realtor and the bank to take it over, finds local people to operate it, helps them furnish it, then services it, and sells it. The company advises on the cash register and the lighting, recommends the texture of the carpet, supplies the Hallmark sign, suggests the color of the walls, and insists on the proper card racks. (Such guidance often was extended to store employees as well. In the 1940s and fifties, in department stores and card shops, Hallmark clerks adhered to a dress code—wearing only black, brown, navy, or charcoal gray—so as not to compete with the merchandise.)

On the fourth floor of Hallmark headquarters in Kansas City, a brief course is conducted for card-store owners. It offers an opportunity to learn the trade from the masters (and is, behind closed doors, nicknamed "Thoughtfulness University"). Owners sign up, pay $500 a week, and attend classes in product display, suggestion selling (translation: you don't wait for questions), insurance, taxes, legal help, local advertising, and public relations. Some retailers return every other year or send recruits.

The company is not a franchiser, nor does it insist that a Hallmark store carry Hallmark cards exclusively, but it carries every Hallmark shop's counter line on the massive computer in Kansas City. This benefits everyone. As Joyce Hall pointed out: "Daily sales reports running into the millions of items indicate whether puppies outsell kittens, how lilacs fare against roses, and whether get-well cards still sell faster in Atlanta than they do in Pittsburgh. Successes or failures are spotted instantly." (Pittsburgh does sell more wedding cards, Silver Anniversary of Your Ordination, First Communion, and Feast Day cards per capita than Atlanta, because more Catholics live in Pittsburgh.)

Based on demographics, location of the store, and its audience, Hallmark can plan and provide the entire line. And replace what need be replaced…by computer. When the pocket of cards in the rack is sold out and the reserve pack depleted, the dealer reorders by sending a computerized form back to Hallmark; from the distribution center in Liberty, Missouri, or Enfield, Connecticut, he receives more of the same card or, if it is no longer available, the card in that category that's the number-one seller.

Joyce C. Hall believed in advertising, too. In 1928, he wrote the company's first full-page ad, which ran in *Ladies' Home Journal*, and that same year the name Hallmark, accompanied by a torch and shield, was introduced on the back of each card. (The torch and shield would be replaced by the five-pointed crown in 1949.) The word "hallmark" intrigued Hall. In the Middle Ages, a hallmark was the official mark of quality stamped on gold and silver pieces produced by Goldsmiths' Hall in London. He made it his mark as well.

Today, there is the *Hallmark Hall of Fame*. And before television there was radio. In 1938, the company sponsored *Tony Wons's Radio Scrapbook*, first on WMAQ in Chicago and then on network in 1940. During the show, chatty Tony would read sentiments from the cards, then say, "Look on the back for the identifying mark—a Hallmark card." When World War II started, so did a Hallmark show called *Meet Your Navy*, with the slogan "Keep 'em Happy With Mail." But no slogan was good enough, not until 1944 when the winner emerged: "When You Care Enough To Send the Very Best." Credit for this has long been accorded a creative vice president named Ed Goodman, a rather reserved chap who deftly blended a couple of phrases provided by Hallmark's advertising agency. The slogan serves its company well. Independent research studies show that it is the most believed advertising slogan in America.

"What we make is bought to be given away," says Bill Johnson, the member of Joyce Hall's ingenious and loyal band who was head of public relations from 1966 to 1985. "And that's a lot different than women's shoes. When you buy shoes, you only have to please one person. When you buy a card, you have to please the sender *and* the recipient." It's Hallmark's job to anticipate the needs of both. But instinct is no longer enough. The planning and design of future lines now rely on other factors.

One is the product information system, a computerized data base put together by analysts in the research department. This is the breakdown of every Hallmark card made over the last five years by its characteristics, and it shows not only what works but also what doesn't. Here, researchers and planners can see retail ratings, number of cards sold, what percent of cards were sent by an individual as opposed to a family or group, how verse has done vs. prose, hot foil vs. flitter, single fold vs. French fold, parchment vs. foilboard, cut-out tip-on vs. acetate overlay, buttons vs. bows. They get the breakdowns of design characteristics such as subject matter—first by categories (florals, animals, insects, inanimate objects, people, scenes), then by types within those categories (roses or zinnias or lilies; ducks, Dalmatians, or doves; lady bugs, butterflies, bees; cupcakes, umbrellas, trains; cupids, couples, clowns; mangers, gardens, villages). And so on.

They also look to the two-hour focus group made up mostly of women (of course, since they buy the most cards), and conducted by qualitative research analysts. Paid participants are selected for their lifestyles: they are married or single, working or not, have children or don't. They are selected for their educations, for where they buy their cards. And they come to talk. They talk about their attitudes toward cards, who they buy them for, what they look for, what gives a card "pickupability." (J. C. Hall felt that if a card didn't get picked up, it didn't have a chance.) They talk about new cards, what they don't like, what they would like to see. Other consumers are questioned in telephone surveys, in panels at the mall.

It is the planners who digest all the research about who buys what card for what reason in which season and know what to do with it. The team wants to offer balance and variety; their purpose is to come up not only with what will sell, but what will mesh. They determine how many new cards to make based on consumer demand from the past, determine new categories (Stepfather/Easter), determine the price points (for Wife/Mother/Sweetheart, men will spend more than for Uncle/Cousin/General Wish, for example, and the closer they are the more they'll spend).

If they are discussing Son Christmas, let us say, for which Hallmark may offer twenty-seven different stock numbers

one year, the team will look at three or four cards from the past five years. They will consider subject matter, color, technique, and format. They will consider the sentiment ("How proud we are," "We seldom say how much we think of you"). In addition to the statistical information, they will study cards next to cards, paneled on cardboard. "One thing we strive to do in all seasons is limit the horizontal cards," adds Wayne Wormsley. "Which is not to say they won't sell. But as a general rule, dealers don't display them horizontally, so people don't pick them up. Also, people aren't used to *opening* cards horizontally."

By analyzing all these components, they put together the next season. "We're not selling a picture," he says. "We're not selling words. We're selling a package. Of our twenty-five thousand employees, we have five to six thousand people involved with different steps of the production of greeting cards. The film, the registration, printing, color separating, die-cutting, packaging, shooting the positives and negatives for lettering, the lettering itself, and so on. Hallmark has always done very well because we try to do things that will appeal to the majority of the people."

Well, almost always. There *have* been a few duds along the way. Another member of Hall's vintage team, Bob McCloskey, recalls the day a designer needed the X-ray of a heart for a card saying, "To show you my heart's in the right place." He went to the doctor. The doctor said, "Sure. There are the files. Help yourself." The designer did. And being no doctor, he chose what McClosky calls "some horrible organ." The picture was printed and in the stores when a customer noticed that it wasn't the heart but the bowels—reproduced upside down. The cards were collected and discarded.

And in 1928, before there was research, there were "Greetaphones." These were plastic phonograph records, two and a half inches across, mounted on cards. You didn't read the sentiment, you spun it. Except that nobody did. "They were a disaster," Joyce Hall lamented, "almost impossible to understand." Customers returned them to the dealers, dealers returned them to Hallmark, Hallmark lost $80,000.

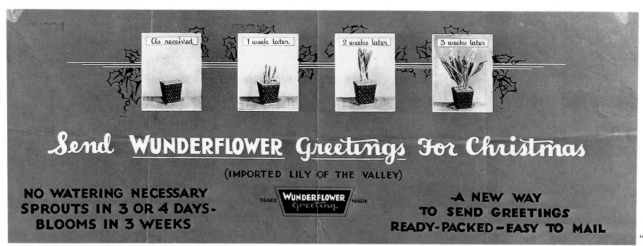

As received | 1 week later | 2 weeks later | 3 weeks later

*Send* **WUNDERFLOWER** *Greetings For Christmas*

(IMPORTED LILY OF THE VALLEY)

NO WATERING NECESSARY
SPROUTS IN 3 OR 4 DAYS-
BLOOMS IN 3 WEEKS

TRADE **WUNDERFLOWER** *Greeting* MARK

-A NEW WAY
TO SEND GREETINGS
READY-PACKED-EASY TO MAIL

*A promotional poster for "Wunderflowers"*

You'd think they would have learned. But for Christmas, 1932, the idea of "Wunderflowers" was, apparently, irresistible. These were potted hunks of moistened peat moss containing lily-of-the-valley pips. The plan was that the bulbs would bloom when they reached room temperature. The problem was that they reached room temperature ahead of schedule when dealers ignored the instructions to keep them in cold storage. In card shops across the nation, thousands of bulbs started sprouting through thousands of packages. For Hallmark, it was not a Merry Christmas.

And even with ten proof-readings, there have been typographical errors. Few will forget the Jewish New Year card with huge Hebrew characters in blue flocking that were printed upside-down or the card that was intended to say "Congratulations on Your New Venture" and, instead, said "Congratulations on Your New Denture."

Winston Churchill, Groucho Marx, Georgia O'Keeffe, Salvador Dali, Andrew Wyeth, Jane Wyman, Norman Rockwell, Grandma Moses, Fred MacMurray, Saul Steinberg, Walt Disney, Henry Fonda, Pablo Picasso, Maurice Utrillo, and Jacqueline Kennedy have all had their art reproduced on Hallmark cards. In 1963, design director Jeannette Lee and Alice Ann Biggerstaff, a longtime Hallmark artist, went to Camp David to visit Mrs. Kennedy. Alice Ann gave her a private lesson, taught her how to apply ink over water-

color instead of watercolor over ink (which she had been doing, and which tended to make the ink run). And Hallmark reproduced and distributed two of her paintings—the three wise men and an exquisite angel—on Christmas cards for the 1963 season to benefit the National Cultural Center.

But most of the art is created in house by Hallmark's staff of designers. In the 1940s, Bob McCloskey, now retired as vice president of international design, was in charge of recruiting Hallmark's artists—about a hundred young men and women a year from America's high schools, junior colleges, and colleges. "J. C. Hall would say, 'Go west,'" he recalls, "and I'd go to towns like Ottawa, Kansas, and Emporia…stop at the high school. I never wrote for appointments ahead of time. The protocol was that I'd go to the principal, not the art teacher. The principal would take me up to meet the art teacher. I'd have to talk to the class about careers and such. When I went to a college, I'd talk to the placement director. I'd move across the country, dip down into Oklahoma, Nebraska, Missouri. If you had the confidence of the head of the school and art department, then kids would flock in.

"We'd have seventy-five to a hundred new people go through the art class, held during the summer term, and if they didn't shape up after the first thirty days, they'd be offered other positions—in color separation or handwork…sewing on buttons, tying bows. The class was taught by Fred Jaeger, who worked in the Hummel style—very Viennese, very successful. You'd get an artist with a flair for a stylized bunny, and Fred would turn to him and say, 'This is an *unpleasant* bunny.'"

The experienced artists did designs for the outside of the card; newcomers—called inside designers—broke in by doing the roses and roosters inside. And in every step along the way, proper procedure prevailed. One 1935 booklet, for example, gives nine long pages of detailed instructions on "How To Make Stencils for Air Brush or Spatter."

Artist Jim Smith remembers how when he first came in 1965, he would be given a ticket, or work order, that stated exactly what he was to do: "A five-to-seven-year-old boy in a workshop situation" or "a five-to-seven-year-old girl on a bicycle." That system continued until the early 1970s, leaving, as he points out, "not a lot of room for freedom of thought." The new system, known as SAC (schedule and control) allows more of it. A project or occasion is first announced in a memo sent through inter-office mail by the planning team to the entire art department or to specific stylists. When convened, the planning team verbally states its needs (Christmas Unlimited, say) and gives a time frame ("Let's work on Christmas for three weeks"), then provides an invaluably detailed hand-out. This is a list of suggested categories (Humorous Better Half, Boss), subjects for illustration (candy canes, elves, reindeer), events (eating falling snowflakes, unwrapping presents), situations (Santa on MTV, animated gingerbread men), format (diecut, popfold), process (emboss, flocking, flitter), styling (art deco, geometric shapes), price points, and colors.

Color trends change in the card game as speedily as they do in the fashion industry. One year it's magenta-red-and-orange, then it's fluorescents, then comes a renaissance of muted roses and raspberries. Holidays have their own rules. Christmas has traditionally called for red and green, Mother's Day for pastel pinks and blues, Halloween for orange—but only Halloween. Except for a brief success in the sixties of an Italian-born orange-and-green-and-yellow combination, orange and green have remained duds as dominant colors.

One expert on animal cards and all other species is Jeannette Lee, who arrived at Hallmark in 1939 as an artist, became design director in 1946 and later vice president, corporate design and a member of the board. She has never worked, nor wanted to work, anywhere else. She says that cute animals—especially kittens and puppies, bunnies and monkeys—appear on more cards than humans do; a drawn picture of a person is never going to look like the recipient anyway. She recalls a period during which Hallmark offered a lot of dachshunds because J. C. Hall had a dachshund. Dogs can be made to look feminine—by using poodles or, as was often done in the 1960s, by dressing the poor creatures in photogenic ruffles. "Cats are cats—they don't look masculine or feminine. And they've become more popular in recent years because of people's independent lifestyles."

"But then," adds Bill Johnson, "all of a sudden you'll have an owl year, a turtle year, a unicorn year." Other creatures that sell well, because they're "safe," are such neuters as elves and cupids. Bears are another story.

"'No bears' was a rule of Mr. Hall's for the longest time," says Lee. "Bears were big and fat, especially in the hips, and he thought they were uncomplimentary to women, particularly mothers. Eventually we did use some bears, but they were like our other animals—cute, with big soft eyes. We

*The art department in the 1940s*

always avoided anything ugly or uncomplimentary, and while some animals may be appealing to a sender, they probably wouldn't be to a recipient." But all rules are made to be broken. With the revived popularity of the Teddy bear in recent years, the bear has been allowed back on the premises and is doing very well indeed.

For ways and means, the artists have Hallmark's creative resource center—a library offering books in open stacks, file upon file of magazine clippings, and volumes showing innumerable styles of borders and ornaments, medals and coins, appliances and costumes, furniture and victuals, flora and fauna. They can also avail themselves of a system known as artwork retrieval, wherein video pictures of art are filed on computer discs and cross-referenced by subject, style, and situation. There are over 40,000 images stored, any of which can be called up when needed. Not only are artists influenced by the seasons and Seventh Avenue; they also read, listen, travel, go to the movies, and watch television, which has certainly made the world more accessible than when J. C. Hall had to window-shop it in person.

With or without research, each artist returns to his or her booth with a hand-out—and a free hand. Gone are the days when directions were dictated and privacy denied, when a flock of artists in a large room sat straight at their desks in tight rows. When the fruits of these labors are harvested, a jury made up of planners, art director, and editorial manager hold a "project review" and select the dandiest designs. The writers see them next and so, when, on the next volley, each artist gets his work order (or ticket), he knows what size the card will be and on what kind of paper it will be printed, how it will fold, what attachments it will carry and, most useful of all, the actual sentiment, its location ("inside right") and tag line ("Happy Birthday")

"Our business is really simple," says Bob McCloskey. "All we have to do is write a sentiment about 100,000 people will want to send another 100,000 people." Not in this business

is a picture worth a thousand words. No matter how irresistible the illustration, people will not buy a card that doesn't say what they want it to say. What's the word that appears most often? *You.*

Verse has always been more popular than prose, although prose is catching up; an innovation known as "conversational verse" falls somewhere in between. In the early days of greeting cards, when roses were red and everything rhymed, publishers and whoever else had the knack and happened to be around often penned their own. Other contributors over the years have included Archibald MacLeish, Boris Pasternak, Phyllis McGinley, Ogden Nash, Charles Dickens, Walt Whitman, Emily Dickinson, Mark Twain, Shakespeare, Keats, Elizabeth Barrett Browning, Ralph Waldo Emerson, and Norman Vincent Peale. But for the most part, it is the in-house writers who keep things in line.

Mary Dorman Lardie, who started at Hallmark in 1934 as an eighteen-year-old artist trainee right out of junior college, became the first official staff writer. She had been around only five months when she heard that the company was setting up an editorial department. Having submitted a few verses even while drawing pen-and-ink border flowers, she decided she'd rather play with words. Her first published verse appeared in 1935:

*I've heard it said*
*Bears go to bed*
*And stay all winter through.*
*But I declare*
*You ain't no bear,*
*So here's my wish for you.*

She kept abreast by reading *The Kansas City Star & Times, The Saturday Evening Post*, and any joke books she could find—and by listening to Bing Crosby, Bob Hope, and the Grand Ole Opry on the radio. While long verse gave her the chance to narrate, as in her wartime card, "A Birthday Letter to My Son In the Service" (one of her favorites), her preferred method was to concoct the punchline and then work up to it in four lines. "Any fool can

A Birthday Letter to My Son
In the Service

Dear Son,

Not many years ago I knew
the perfect joy
That comes to every mother
of a little baby boy
I said a little prayer for
strength and wisdom, too, to see
Just how to make my boy the
boy I hoped that he would be.
Your father was so proud of you,
that, really I'm not joking
He gave enough cigars away
to keep the whole town smoking.

We thought you were a wonder child, and, Son, to tell the truth,
We almost sent out telegrams when you got your first tooth.
We were so proud of things you'd do, and cute things you would say
That how you kept from being spoiled I don't know to this day.
The weeks and months grew into years, the years passed one by one
And only brought more reasons to be prouder of you, Son.
And sometimes when things went all wrong, I longed to baby you
But that's among the things a mother soon learns not to do.
And now it means so very much to see you strong and fine
The brave young man who used to be that little

We mothers have to stay at home, but we keep busy, too,
And everything that I have done has been for boys like you.
But buying bonds and
Red Cross work and
pastimes we're pursuing
Seem almost nothing, Son,
compared to what you
boys are doing.
So please forgive your Mom today if she's been sentimental,
And there's no reason to pretend that it's been accidental
I've just been reminiscing, as a Mother's apt to do
And in my heart I said a prayer that all is well with you.
And in my heart I said a prayer that all is well with you.
I'll close with Happy Birthday and a hope you'll be home soon—
I'll bake you a great big
birthday cake and let you
sleep till noon!

With all my love,

write things long," she says today—from her cherry or-chard in northern Michigan—"but it takes skill and know-how to write things short."

In Lardie's day, an assignment went from the planning committee to Charles Christian Culp, her editor, to her. Today's staff writers receive their assignments on requisition sheets. "There is presently a dearth of Religious Concern-Cope sentiments," reads one for a Friendship Writing Project. "We especially need long conventional prose and 6-line (and longer) verse that compliments the recipient's resourcefulness, offers reassurance of God's care, and/or reminds the recipient of other trials safely conquered by faith. Bible ref. okay."

And this, on a Cheery Writing Project: "We need *lots* of serious copy—mostly medium-length prose, some verse—in Hospital, Operation, Seriously Ill, Masculine, and multiple sender captions like Our Wish, From Both, and From All....On the lighter side, we also need humor ideas (as always), especially for Hospital and Operation. Are there any *new* jokes about hospitals—not nurses, gowns, food, or expenses—or new angles to the old standbys? How about copy-on-cover ideas with a design payoff *inside* for a change?"

Dean Walley was a journalism major at the University of Missouri before joining Hallmark. Now one of the senior writers, he's also the man who offers a marvelous course in American manners—and manners of speaking—to the artists and writers. Projecting slides of old cards from Hallmark's archives on a small screen, he will rhapsodize on a colloquialism here, chuckle at an antiquated idea there, applaud an adjective, blast a dialect. He loves the high-falutin' use of the word "grand," the bravado of "staunch," the evasiveness of "To a certain cheerful some-one." His sentimental olio embraces cards of every era, every province: a bluebird of the twenties chirping "Please Hurry Back," a Dutch girl saying "To mine friend," a tippler saying "Happy Birschday to You," greetings to the dentist, a quack from Donald Duck. The point is that Hallmark writers must keep up with the language as it changes. O tempera! O mores!

Everything's up to date in Kansas City. Hallmark headquarters is not only an exceptionally gracious workplace—which is, of course, as it should be—it is also exceptionally efficient. Completed in 1956, the complex occupies fifteen acres and more than two million square feet. It is adjacent to Crown Center, the $500-million eighty-five acre complex developed by Hallmark and designed by Edward Larrabee Barnes to revitalize the inner city.

The main building is, in shape, an inverted pyramid built into the side of a hill. With Hopper, Sheeler, and Frankenthaler on the walls and a receiving dock on every floor to eliminate the need (and delay) of elevators, this is the hub of all planning and creativity. Here, too, in a hangar-sized space piled high with lithographed sheets, is where cards are cut apart, die-cut, and embossed after they have been printed in production centers scattered throughout Kansas and Missouri. Annual sales are more than $2 billion, and cards are only the half of it. Hallmark also produces gift wrap, ribbon, party goods, calendars, posters, toys, ornaments, jigsaw puzzles, picture frames, photo albums, books, candles, mugs, pens, pencils, stationery, jewelry, pewter plates, and porcelain figurines—and owns Binney & Smith, the maker of Crayola crayons.

Until late in his seventies, J. C. Hall personally approved every new card. His all-time favorite was the best-selling pansy card, and his favorite message was "My Friend" by Edgar Guest. When he was in his eighties, and semi-retired, he was still driving to work two or three days a week in one of his two 1963 Buicks.

In 1982, Joyce C. Hall—Commander of the Order of the British Empire, holder of the French Legion of Honor, winner of the Eisenhower Medallion, winner of the first Emmy awarded to a television sponsor, and recipient of the Horatio Alger award among many others—died at the age of 91. His beloved company is still privately held; the Hall family owns about 67 percent of the stock, and the employees own the rest. Irvine O. Hockaday, Jr. (who was, like J. C., born in the popular month of August) is president and chief executive officer. Joyce Hall's son, Donald Joyce Hall, is chairman of the board.

*The "Okay Committee," presided over by Joyce C. Hall, approved every card*

The ups and downs of our economy, our hemlines, and our mood: such is the grist for the Hallmark mill. The days of our lives, as you will see on the following pages, are reflected in the cards of our days. Prohibition, fitness, the income tax, Vietnam, the G-man, the G.O.P., women's suffrage, women's lib, the radio, the jukebox, the computer, talkies, hula hoops, the Atom bomb, the gray flannel suit, the mini skirt, *My Fair Lady*, Huey Long, Mickey Mouse, the TV quiz show, the fireside chat, the Duchess of Windsor, Miss Piggy, Sputnik, the beatnik, Charlie Brown, Charles Lindbergh, canasta, Mussolini, rationing, cowboys, hippies, hillbillies, bobby soxers, flappers, the Dionne Quints, Valley Girls, the airplane, the blackout, the Crash. The seasons come, the seasons go, and Hallmark is up to the minute.

"Actually," says Bill Johnson, "most cards reflect more everyday life than national events. And a national event does not in itself bring about a card. Most are ignored by the greeting-card industry. It would be folly to pretend that by looking at cards from 1920 to 1935, say, you'd get a full idea of what was going on in America." But you get a pretty good one.

The Depression stirred people long settled. Many left their southern farms and migrated to the Rust Belt (cities like Gary, Detroit, Pittsburgh) and the industrial north. Thus followed cards to the old folks at home—as well as to the teachers, ministers, doctors, and coffee klatschers. After World War II, when our boys came home, Americans moved again. Some draftees fell in love with the states to which they'd been assigned, some fell in love with girls to whom they became wed, and some, thanks to the GI Bill, went off to college. All such leave-takings prompted streams of greeting cards across the miles.

Although patriotic cards fell off instantly as soon as peace was declared, many soldiers had by then become converts. With melancholy memories of mail call, they well knew the comfort cards could provide. And so they became customers (not such good customers as women, of course, who ordinarily send about 90 percent of all cards, but better than they had been). Men buy for birthdays, Valentine's Day, and Christmas, and especially for Mother's Day, which is the only holiday for which they buy more cards than women.

In the twenties, cards for Mom were floral, respectful, loving. In the thirties, forties, and fifties, they were reflections of her domesticity—but not her drudgery. When, in the sixties, some Moms decided they couldn't stand the heat and got out of the kitchen, Mother's Day cards began to reflect their moves from the stove to the desk, lugging briefcases instead of vacuum cleaners.

Dads have changed, too. Gone, pretty much, is the Father's Day image of The Man in his easy chair, the newspaper in his hands, the dog at his feet, the smoking pipe between his firm lips. In these days of shared domes-ticity, the cards may show him in the kitchen, in the garden, toting a baby in a back pack. But the cards are fewer and fewer. Just as television has reduced the world's need of bridge talleys, which once bulked large in Hallmark's inventory, so have divorce, abortion, and single-parent families increasingly made Dad a missing person. Ironically, although he has come to appreciate the greeting card more than he once did, today's father—often no longer a member of the household—doesn't even expect a card on Father's Day.

Whatever the season, birthday cards remain the most constant enticement. There is one to commemorate a first birthday and one for a 100th birthday, even one to say Happy Birthday from a pet. There are cards for the least official events conceivable—You're a Big Brother Now, A Job Well Done, congratulations on getting braces, stopping smoking, adopting a baby, a successful diet. People are marrying later, or they're getting divorced (and sending out an announcement), or they're staying single. They're having babies later, and fewer of them. The po' working girl has become an executive assistant. Santa and the stork have lost their credibility.

But never mind. Here, in a glorious romp through the envelopes of the past, is the very best that Americans have cared to send. Clearly, it is *not* more blessed to give than to receive. Not in this case.

*Hall Brothers picnic, 1921. Joyce C. Hall is standing fourth from the far right*

Just a Great Big Wish for A Merry Christmas for OUR BIG BOY

*c. 1929*

"Our Big Boy" looked suspiciously like "Our Little Sweetheart" in these two cards from the 1920s. Sure, the artist was taking a shortcut, but didn't the public notice?

Just a Great Big Wish for A MERRY CHRISTMAS for Our Little Sweetheart

*c. 1929*

Bringing~ A VALENTINE to my LITTLE FRIEND

*1929*

# Scenes from Childhood

They've had their gods—Buck Rogers in the air, Bill Stern *on* the air, Davy Crockett and Sonny Crockett, Hopalong and Howdy, Superman and Dillinger, Jack Armstrong and Jackie Robinson. And they've held the prizes—the Dick Tracy badges, Tootsie Toy rocket ships, Tom Mix rings, Shirley Temple dolls, Barbie dolls, Little Orphan Annie mugs, Big Little Books. And, despite their age of innocence, they've also knitted socks for the soldiers, collected scrap metal and sacrificed bubblegum, played a Depression game called Eviction, and dug bomb shelters. Here's looking at you, kids.

VALENTINE GREETINGS

TO MY PLAYMATE
To wish you happiness on Valentine's Day!

1928

BRINGING—
A VALENTINE TO MY LITTLE FRIEND

1929

*1944*

*1939*

*1987*

**Boys and Girls Together**

*1939*

*1986*

*1942*

*1935*

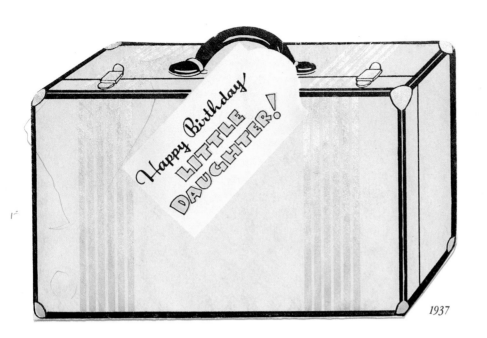

*1937*

This little cut-up of the thirties was the ingenuous ancestor of the fifties' Mary Lou and the eighties' Becky Sue.

PARTY DRESS

SCHOOL DRESS

PLAY DRESS

PAJAMAS

COAT

THIS LITTLE DOLLY PACKED
HER GRIP
AND CAME TO PLAY WITH YOU,
AND SINCE YOU'RE JUST SO DEAR
AND SWEET
SHE'S GOING TO STAY WITH
You!

1934

1949

1935

Little women

For a Sweet Niece

1939

1929

1987

1929

1936

1940

Little men

In 1947, Hallmark published Dolls from the Land of Make Believe (of which Cinderella was the favorite), a year later, Dolls of the Nations, and a year later still *Little Women* Dolls. A special Collector's Album was available for each series. Card buyers were told that the *"Little Women* Dolls were sketched from life by Hallmark artists on the set of the new Metro-Goldwyn-Mayer technicolor production *Little Women,"* but the dolls' faces were identical.

1947

1947

1947

1947

1949

1948

1948

1948

GREETINGS for EASTER

*1929*

*1987*

# An Animal Kingdom

I n the card game, cats and dogs are the beasts that sell best. Kittens and puppies sell better than big ones, and white kittens sell better than brown kittens. Dogs—especially poodles, dachshunds, and cocker spaniels, which are considered "loving," as opposed to shepherds and bulldogs, which are not—*used* to sell better than cats. But, thanks to the single life and the working woman, cats are now the cat's pajamas. They can stay home alone all day. They are convenient. They are cozy. Cozy, cuddly, and cute are what all Hallmark animals must be—the rabbits, monkeys, bears, lambs, ducks, mice, chipmunks...even the occasional snake, skunk, dinosaur, and dragon—because they must never be unflattering to the recipient (especially Mom).

*1936*  A HAPPY EASTER TO SOMEONE NICE

A Hallmark
Menagerie:
The Twenties &
Thirties

The bunny, top right, is
kept aloft by a real
piece of candy. The
bear, bottom right, is
one of the few that
Joyce Hall—who felt
bears were unpleasant
on cards—let out of
its cage.

*I may not be in WHO'S
WHO but...
But I know WHAT'S WHAT
I wanta be Your
Valentine and THAT'S
THAT!

1929

*This bunny is flying to You
with sweet EASTER Greetings*

c. 1929

PLEASE HURRY BACK

When you're away I'm plenty blue—
The bluest bird you ever knew
Blue as the ocean's deepest hues
Bluer than the blueing laundries use—
Bluer than you can ever know
Please hurry back—I miss you so!

1929

Here's a DUCKY little greeting
just to wish you
HAPPY EASTER

1929

I may not be in ~
WHO'S WHO
but ~

*1929

Ether you're my VALENTINE~
or I'm full of static

1928

Here's a chick little greeting to wish
YOU a happy EASTER

1928

WE'RE NOT HERE TO ARGUE
WE'RE SIMPLY HERE TO SAY:—
WE HOPE YOU HAVE A HOWLING TIME
AT YOUR HOUSE CHRISTMAS DAY.

1925

DON'T YOU
THINK I'D
MAKE A
BEAR OF A
VALENTINE?

c. 1929

*1932*

Joyce Hall began to use Disney characters on his cards in 1932—he was the first licensee. Walt Disney, who had lived in Kansas City from 1910 to 1923, was to become a good friend of Hall's. On cards, as on the screen, Minnie, Mickey, Donald, and their friends, have changed in appearance over the years.

1935

1934

1940

**A Hallmark
Menagerie:
The Thirties**

The scottie was
certainly inspired by
F.D.R.'s famous pet,
Fala.

1929

1939

Early 1930s

1932

1937

1940

1942

1944

1954

c. 1963

A Hallmark
Menagerie:
The Forties, Fifties &
Sixties

1940

1944

1965

1942

The wartime chick
came in red, white, and
blue. By the
fifties, the hare
was debonair.
According to Hallmark's
Jeanette Lee, the
anthropomorphic rabbit
"animates well, has
expressive ears, and is
very cuddly."

The world's most famous beagle entered the scene in the early fifties.

*1974*

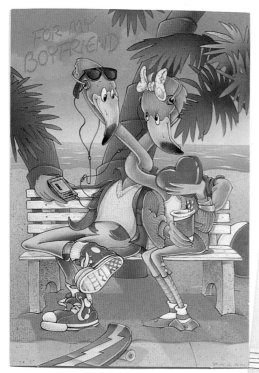

*1987*

*1987*

*1987*

A Hallmark
Menagerie:
The Eighties

*1987*

*1987*

*1987*

# The Teen Age

Once upon a time, they were adolescents. Then, around World War II, they became teenagers, earning the wages and acquiring status. While some girls stayed in, babysitting for mothers on the night shift, others went out. Brenda Frazier, flouncing through the nightclubs of the thirties, was a teenager—and so was Andy Hardy. They wore saddle shoes and bobby sox, army boots and dungarees. They danced the jitterbug, the bop, and the twist; swung with Benny Goodman, sung with Sinatra, fainted for Elvis, screamed for the Beatles. They jerked sodas and spoke jive, smooched at the drive-in, read *Mad* and *Modern Screen*, watched too much television, and were convinced they knew it all.

Like y'know
Like it's no biggie.
Like y'know,
Nothing awesome,
I mean like,
I just want to
Like say hello,
totally
fer sure.

*1984*

*1942*

Three little maids from school: in the forties, they met for malteds; in the eighties, they hang out at the mall.

*1945*

*1942*

*1939*

*1942*

**Brat Pack: The Forties**

The war was over and life was a party. Hallmark discovered teenagers, and teenage slang, but was sometimes off the mark. "Perf, geetchie, cagey, snazzy, sharp": did *anybody* ever talk that way?

*1939*

*1946*

*1949*

*1971

*Some things turn me off,
it's true...
But I sure turn on when I
think of you!

1969

SIS--
You're
GROOVY,
TERRIFIC,
a SWINGER,
real GONE...

For a Fine Nephew
Nothing too
"hip"
Very "in"
or
"offbeat"--

1971

1971

GRANDSON,
IT'S YOUR
BIRTHDAY,
SO DO
YOUR
OWN
THING--

1971

FOR A
DAUGHTER
WHO IS
EVERYTHING
W
O
N
D
E
R
F
U
L

You're Sweet
Sixteen!

Girls who are
as sweet
as you
Are few
and far
between--

It's the talk of
the TOWN,
So
you really
should know--

1967

Here it is... An
"OLDIE-BUT-
GOODIE"--

1970

ON THE SUBJECT OF SISTERS
There's not much
you can do about 'em--

1956

1970

**Brat Pack: The Fifties,
Sixties & Seventies**

Ponytails, Beatle cuts,
sideburns. Nobody
wanted them, but they
had each other.

1981

1981

1984

## Brat Pack: The Eighties

The wheel turns: "Brother, UR Super, Cool, Tops, Xlent, Tuff, Nice, Fun, Gr8."

1987

1987

1987

1984

1986

35

# *After School*

In the ivied years of the past, Joe College rushed a fraternity, sat on a flagpole, played on the team, went to the prom, majored in something or other, and graduated into a gray flannel suit and a job on the Street. Today, he—and Betty Coed—join the rat race. To celebrate this rite of passage, we will send them (as well as their siblings graduating from nursery school, kindergarten, grade school, junior high, high school, and graduate school) about 85 million cards this year.

*To a Sweet Girl Graduate*

1932

*You're graduating?
...from a school?

* 1958

36

IF YOU'RE NOT THE **NEATEST**, **SHARPEST**, MOST **TERRIFIC** GRADUATE AROUND...

*1971*

I hear you're getting up in the world!
CONGRATULATIONS, GRADUATE

*1933*

Congratulations you've got yourself a bachelor's degree...

*1958*

CONGRATULATIONS!
AND MAY YOUR LOFTIEST DREAMS COME TRUE.

*1958*

*1962*

Graduated?
That certainly gets my STAMP of APPROVAL!
OK

CONGRATULATIONS!

*1932*

CONGRATULATIONS GIRL GRADUATE!

KNOW YOU'RE HEADED FOR A GREAT CAREER!!

*1959*

*Congratulations
You've got yourself a
bachelor's degree...
Now, go get yourself a
bachelor!*

Thanks for Remembering my Graduation
Your kind remembrance
Surely ranks
As the thrill of a
lifetime
Many Thanks

*1928*

TO THE Grade School Graduate
CAT 2+2 ABC

*1959*

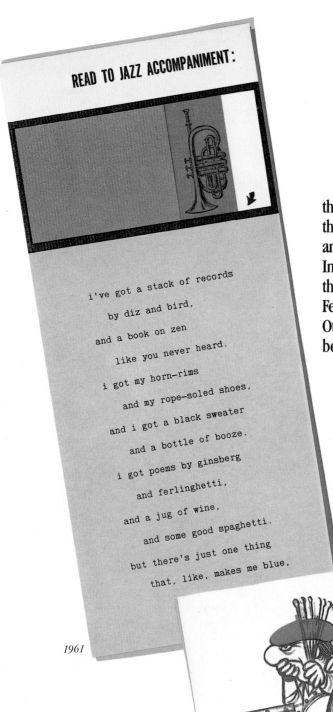

i've got a stack of records
by diz and bird,
and a book on zen
like you never heard.
i got my horn-rims
and my rope-soled shoes,
and i got a black sweater
and a bottle of booze.
i got poems by ginsberg
and ferlinghetti,
and a jug of wine,
and some good spaghetti.
but there's just one thing
that, like, makes me blue,

*1961*

# Beatniks

Every age has its rebel band, and the 1950s—a time of awesome prosperity and materialism—had the Beats. They spouted Zen and sported beards, dressed in black and strummed the blues, smoked pot and shared pipe dreams. Instead of going to work, they hung out in coffeehouses or back at the pad. They dug cats like Kerouac and Corso, Miles and Monk, Ferlinghetti and Ginsburg. And they dug chicks. Who were they? Other mothers' sons—immersed in beatitude, feeling their own beat, on any road but the beaten path.

*\* 1958*

*\*The group just isn't SOLID without you!*

*Me and my chick wish you a
Happy Birthday!

*1960

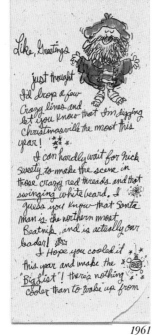

*Me and my chick wish you a
Happy Birthday!

*1960

1960

*Like, Greetings... Just thought I'd drop a few crazy lines and let you know that I'm digging Christmasville the most this year!* I can hardly wait for Nick sweety, to make the scene in those crazy red threads and that swinging white beard. I guess you know that Santa man is the northern most Beatnik, and is actually our leader. I hope you cooled it this year and make the "Big List"! there's nothing cooler than to wake up from

1961

I aM a MEMBER
OF THE BEAT
GENERATION

PROBLEMS

1960

Hey man....
conformity got
you bugged?
Then cut loose
and live the
life of the free
inner man!!!
Right here is
all you need
to be a genuine
BEATNICK!!!!

1961

*Absinthe...makes the heart grow
fonder

be-Bopa-doo
Be-bopa-doo

FRiM-FraM-a-Rebop
a-Scooby-doo

ooPoPa-dee
ooPoPa-dow

Heybob-a-Reba
a-SHooby-do-ow

1960

LiKe, HaPPY
FaTHER'S
daY....

ZEN

1961

FOR THE
DiScRiMiNaTiNG PERSON,
aN aUTHeNTiC
FOLK MUSiC
BiRTHDaY
CaRD!

1965

LiKe,
IN a
LiTTLE
WHiLE....

* 1962

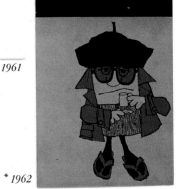

*Like, in a little while...
You'll be gone man!! 'Bye!!

# 𝓗𝑎𝑝𝑝𝑦 𝓑𝑖𝑟𝑡ℎ𝑑𝑎𝑦

Joyce C. Hall wasn't the only kid born in August. So were Andy Warhol, Ogden Nash, Robert Redford, Robert Mitchum, Herbert Hoover, Eddie Fisher, Norma Shearer, Bert Lahr, Annie Oakley, Julia Child, Mae West, Bernard Baruch, Wilt Chamberlain, Ingrid Bergman, Leonard Bernstein, Count Basie, Gene Kelly, Ruby Keeler, Michael Jackson, Alfred Hitchcock, Arthur Godfrey, Caligula, and LBJ. It's the most popular birthday month of the year. Least popular: February (it's the shortest) and April (it's the cruelest).

1927

To hope your birthday
is a WOW!
(Please overlook the slang)
A happy, happy day ~ ~
AND HOW!
Sincerely yours,
The Gang

*1936*

*1942*

*1938*

*1981*

*1959*

*1944*

*1940*

*1982*

*1933*

*1943*

*1987*

*1944*

Party Lines:
The Twenties &
Thirties

IT'S A WHALE OF A WISH FOR A HAPPY BIRTHDAY

THIS IS NO FISH TAIL

*1929*

A HAPPY BIRTHDAY to Our Little Sweetheart

*1929*

SIX YEARS OLD Happy Birthday

*1930*

For A Happy Birthday

*1930*

BABY'S first BIRTHDAY

*1931*

HAPPY BIRTHDAY

*1930*

*1931*

Five Years Old HAPPY BIRTHDAY

Late 1920s

DOLLY AND I BOTH WISH YOU A HAPPY BIRTHDAY

*1927*

See if you can BLOW A NOTE

*1932*

*1928*

I've Got Your Number ~ HAPPY BIRTHDAY

My tale is short Happy Birthday

44

*1935*

*1930*

*1932*

Party Lines:
The Thirties

*1938*

*1935*

*1935*

*1932*

*1933*

*1931*

*1931*

*1935*

You couldn't get a drink, but you could still say "Hell" on a greeting card. By the fifties, it would be just the opposite.

*1931*

*1934*

*1934*

*1933*

*1931*

*1937*

Party Lines:
The Thirties

Some topical themes here: The Dionne Quintuplets...and birth control, G-men and Huey Long. Not to mention the Duke of Windsor ("Don't worry about birthdays, if you "like 'em"—well, that's great! But if you don't...The thing to do is up and abdicate!").

*1935*

*1935*

*Birthday Greetings*
LET'S "STAMP" OUT THE DICTATORS!

*1942*

But, WHAT THE HECK,
THEY CAN BE FUN--
IT'S ALL IN HOW
YOU TAKE 'EM!!
*Happy Birthday!*

*About These Birthdays*
THEY'RE JUST LIKE TRAVELIN' SALESMEN,
IT'S SURE PLENTY HARD TO SHAKE 'EM

*1949*

**Party Lines:
The Forties**

While some made hay, the war made headlines—even on birthday cards.

WELL, BLOW MY HORN AND CALL ME TOOTS!
IT'S YOUR BIRTHDAY!

*1941*

*1941*

*Birthday Greetings to the* TWINS
a "double" birthday, no mistake?

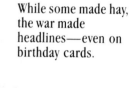

*1944*

HOW

GREAT WHITE FATHER, F.D.R.,
HE GIVE-UM FIRESIDE CHAT
HE SAY WE NOW MUST WIN-UM WAR
AND ALL-UM STUFF LIKE THAT.

*1946*

BIRTHDAY GREETINGS
TO SOMEONE WHO WON'T WRITE

Supposin' you *have* got a birthday?
The way I've been treated by you,
Why should I care if it's happy or not?--
I sure don't know why--

*1940*

*Happy Birthday*
TO A SWEET LITTLE GIRL

A HAPPY BIRTHDAY
TO A BIG BOY

*1940*

Party Lines:
The Forties

ON
CARS
AND
TIRES
AND
HOSE,

BUT THERE IS SURE NO
**SHORTAGE** NOW
ON <u>WISHES</u>, YOU CAN BET,
SO HERE'S A <u>WORLD</u>
OF WISHES
FOR YOUR
**HAPPIEST BIRTHDAY**
YET!

*Birthday Greetings to You in the* W.A.C.

*1943*

HAPPY BIRTHDAY

*1941*

BIRTHDAY GREETINGS

THERE'S A SHORTAGE NOW ON LOTS OF THINGS AS EVERYBODY KNOWS, ON **GASOLINE**

**ALUMINUM**

*1941*

HELLO THERE

Hope your Birthday's a Cracker Jack

*1940*

Any scarcity—of cash or gas, booze or hose—permits Hallmark's writers to emphasize the abundance of good wishes.

*Well, knock me over the fence and call me* HOMER,

*1941*

THEY CAN HAVE BLACKOUTS

FROM SEA TO SEA,

*1943*

Hope Your Birthday's a Winner

Don't want to argue politics—I only want to say:

HAPPY BIRTHDAY
(WAR TIME SAVING TIME)

YOU MAY NOT LIKE THE EARLY HOURS THIS WAR TIME SAVING BRINGS, IT MAY BE INCONVENIENT (THAT'S THE WAY WITH ALL THESE THINGS)

*1942*

BIRTHDAY GREETINGS FROM YOUR SECRET PAL

*Who sent this card is something I can't reveal, of course.*

*1942*

*1957*

Party Lines:
The Fifties

*1956*

*1957*

The TV we bought on the installment plan brought us that notorious skinflint, Jack Benny, and that granddaddy of quiz shows, *What's My Line*, as well as rumblings of a more troubled world. And who could fail to finish the line, "you ain't nuthin' but a..."?

*1959*

*1956*

*1959*

*1958*

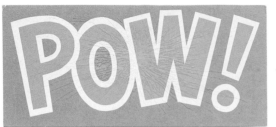

1966

1960s

when it comes to our family's Genealogy...

1984

Happy Birthday

...to a real cute number!

1960

AT OUR AGE... | ...NOT MUCH CAN GO WRONG... | ...THERE ARE SO FEW MOVING PARTS.

HAPPY BIRTHDAY!

1976

**Party Lines:
The Sixties, Seventies
& Eighties**

HERE'S A GENUINE SPACE AGE BIRTHDAY GIFT FOR YOU ... AN ACTUAL NOSE CONE !

1965

On Our Birthday
Since we always share a birthday, let's share the commemorating...

1987

Did anyone ASK you if you wanted to be a year older? Of COURSE not! Well, don't you think that's UNFAIR? Don't you think that's a violation of your RIGHTS? Of COURSE it is! Well, DO something about it! It's time for ACTION! PROTEST!! DO IT NOW!!

1967

# All for Love

We have, in our time, been bewitched, bothered, and bewildered by computer dating and a chase through the classifieds. So much for function, but whither form? Cyrano, Romeo, Lothario, and Porfirio knew what a girl likes best: ravishing words and *billets doux,* roses are red and violets are blue. Hallmark happens to know it, too.

To M**RU**SH Valentine

TAG!
My Valentine
You're it

1929

A 1926 *Saturday Evening Post* cover by Norman Rockwell was the inspiration for these childhood sweethearts.

NEXT TO MYSELF
I LIKE YOU BEST

1931

Early 1930s

Two by two

From Lover's Lane to the fast lane, the models may have changed but the national pastime has not.

1987

*1987*

*1985*

*1935*

*1930*

*1966*

SWEETHEART, You've got me...

*1973*

How'd Ya Like to be MY VALENTINE?

*Where it comes, now, to wooin'
Do I know what's doin'?*

*1944*

In the twenties and thirties, they waltzed, they wooed, they wed. Today, love is more casual. The eighties couple on the park bench haven't even become acquainted …yet.

*1934*

BABY...

A Christmas Greeting
FOR MY SWEETHEART

Valentine Greetings
TO SOMEONE I LOVE

*1934*

* 1959

* Let's go out together.

1984

Two's company; one's
half a date...

...and a girl can't be too bashful.

1942

BOYS HARDLY EVER WHISTLE MUCH WHEN I GO WALKING BY,

COPYRIGHT 1942, HALL BROTHERS, INC.

THEY DON'T SAY, "HI YA, TOOTS!" TO ME AND WINK A WICKED EYE,

I'M NOT THE KIND TO MAKE 'EM STOP AND TURN AROUND AND STARE,

I'M NOT SO HOT — — BUT JUST THE SAME,

I AIN'T NO FRIGIDAIRE!

Forward passes: a gallery of pushy gals.

*I don't know what I was thinking of—to get you an affectionate type friendship card like this... Like to guess?

*1960

1928

1972

1960

1935

56

1960

1952

I WANT A SINGLE MAN!

THINK IT OVER

1935

1984

Aw Gee - I guess I'm just one of those girls that men forget

1928

1985

You're~
My VALENTINE

*1929*

It must be LOVE!

*1931*

Don't
LOCK
me
out of
your *heart*~
I want to be
your Valentine!

*1928*

Hearts:
The Twenties &
Thirties

For My Valentine

*1928*

Is it SAFE~TA~PIN my faith
in you
And choose you ~ for my
VALENTINE

*1928*

Just *hunting* for
A VALENTINE

*1929*

Don't *kid* me
BE MY
VALENTINE

*1929*

Excuse me for *button*~in
but *gosh* ~ I want You for my VALENTINE

*1928*

Just BUTTON
with a big wi
for a happy
VALENTINE'S
Day~for
YOU

*1929*

58

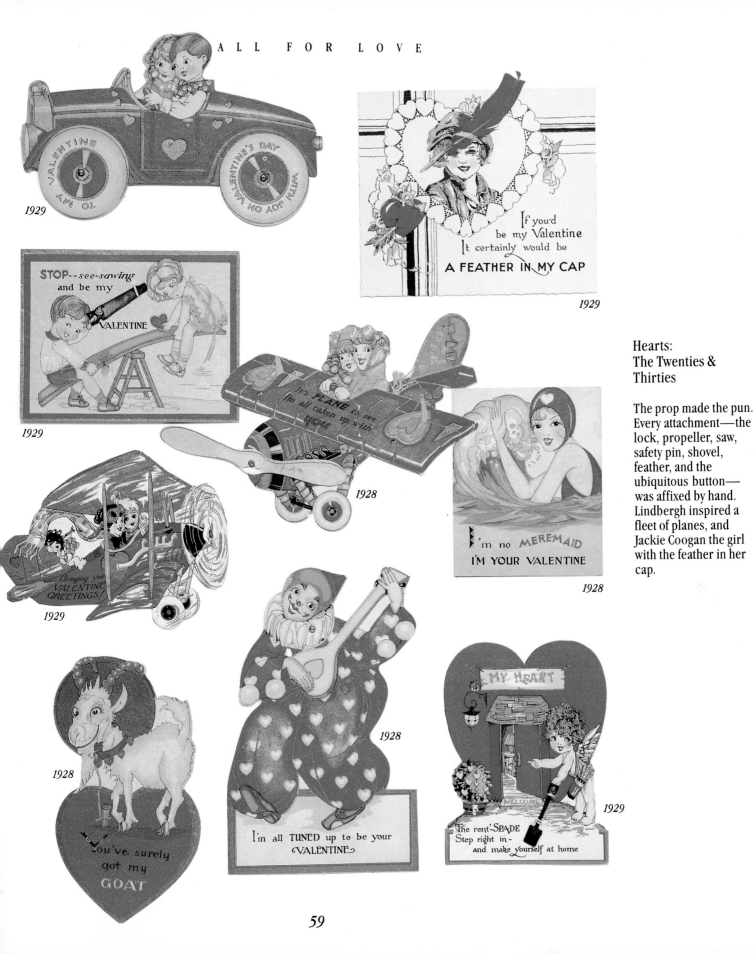

*1929*

*1929*

*1929*

*1929*

*1928*

*1928*

*1928*

*1928*

*1928*

*1929*

**Hearts:
The Twenties &
Thirties**

The prop made the pun.
Every attachment—the
lock, propeller, saw,
safety pin, shovel,
feather, and the
ubiquitous button—
was affixed by hand.
Lindbergh inspired a
fleet of planes, and
Jackie Coogan the girl
with the feather in her
cap.

Banks are full of MONEY~

Dogs are full of FLEAS~

Cities are full of

GANGSTERS!

*1931

I HOPE YOU'LL BE MY VALENTINE

YOU'RE ALL THE STIMULANT I need!

1931

A Valentine for You Mother dear

1928

A VALENTINE With lots of love for OUR BIG BOY

1931

A VALENTINE With Lots of Love

for OUR LITTLE SWEETHEART

1932

Hearts:
The Twenties &
Thirties

*Banks are full of MONEY—
Dogs are full of FLEAS—
Cities are full of
GANGSTERS!—
Hives are full of BEES—
Fords are full of
RATTLES—
Music's full of TUNES—
and
If you won't be MY
VALENTINE —
I think you're FULL OF
PRUNES!

LET'S NOT MONKEY AROUND~LET'S MAKE UP!

c. 1930

Hello DADDY I'm Your VALENTINE!

1929

VALENTINE GREETINGS
Why Don't You Write?

Have you so many fish to fry
You cannot write as days go by?
So many other things to do
You can't dash off a line or two?
Is life so busy you can't squeeze
A word or two in edgewise~
please? ~ ~ Take notice
of this Valentine
And send me anyhow~
~ a line

1928

VALENTINE GREETINGS
TO MY NEW~FOUND FRIEND

Since I am not an old friend
Who's known you for some years
You may think I'm a bold friend
When this Valentine appears
But though you are a new friend
I'm as glad as I can be
To count you as a true friend
In every way to me

60

WARNING!
*This Valentine's
from a Married Woman*

*1931*

UR THE **FLOUR** OF
**MY** ♥ **HEART**
♥ SWEET ♥ VALENTINE

HEARTY ♥ MILLS LTD.
SUGARTON ON THE HUDSON
TRADE MARK

*1932*

FOR
VALENTINE'S DAY
Roses are not
always red .....
Violets not
always blue
But...
sugar's always very sweet ...
And
so
are ..... YOU!

*1929*

BORED
AND
ROOM

*For* ~~
A NICE VALENTINE!

*1931*

Hearts:
The Twenties &
Thirties

Once upon a time,
people made their own
music. People lived in
rooming houses. People
baked their own bread,
too. But the best-known
valentine verse still
dwells on roses, violets,
sugar, and you.

If you'd
say you'd be
MY
VALENTINE ... It sure would be
*Sweet Music*
to my ears

*1933*

A VALENTINE FOR DAUGHTER

*1938*

*1931*

Take a
swing with me
and be my
VALENTINE

I'll be reduced to tears
If you won't be
MY VALENTINE!

*1931*

Hearts:
The Forties

A Valentine For A Certain Sailor

Some girls may go for soldiers, I know lots of them do—

But when it comes to Valentines, I go for NAVY BLUE!

1942

Valentine Message For You

This is just a SAMPLE of how broken up I'll be

If you won't say you're willing to be VALENTINES with ME!

1940s

A Valentine Message From Someone Who Cares.

1946

"A Special Valentine for You"

1945

1945

Here's an early jigsaw puzzle, suggesting just how far Hallmark would go to piece together a pun.

1944

To my Husband With Love on Valentine's Day

1942

HIYA, SOLDIER!

Just thought I'd better let you know In case you're kinda shy

TO MY SWEETHEART On Valentine's Day

The schmaltzy valentine:
He spent a little extra on
this one.

c. 1950

*1962*

## Hearts:
## The Fifties

The little Cockney in the flowered hat—Eliza Doolittle?—yawps, "'ow 'bout it?" The voluptuous bridge player is vulnerable, "if you're game!" And who cares if mothers are against kissing? "I don't want to kiss your mother."

*1958*

*1958*

*1958*

*1959*

*1957*

*1952*

*1962*

*1961*

*1960*

*1960*

*1960*

*1968*

Hearts:
The Sixties

*1961*

*1962*

*1973*

*1962*

For some, Hugh Hefner
and his bunny replaced
Romeo and Juliet as
symbols of true love—
or was it just true sex?

1987

Hearts:
The Seventies
& Eighties

1987

1987

How about a pajama party on Valentine's Day?

There's something very exciting
about your hand reaching
out to mine...
Something very comfortable
about having someone
who knows me so completely...

1987

1987

i love you

1987

1987

FOR A VERY NICE
BABYSITTER

I ♥
LIKE
YOU!
xo

1981

1987

# Under the Weather

ake your medicine, get your sleep, and open your mail. Generations of invalids have been cheered by bedridden puppy dogs, out-of-tune pianos, and sputtering jalopies in need of repair. Year after year, epidemic after epidemic, such popular tonics have nursed us through chicken pox and tonsilitis, measles and mumps, the common cold and the broken leg. They have found us in stitches (and kept us in stitches), hoped to see us back at the office soon, urged us to feel fit as a fiddle, full of beans, in mint condition, in fine feather, and like a million bucks. And more likely than not, they have actually wished us well.

1930

HURRY AND GET WELL

Rx
Don't know
what the doctor
ordered
To help you while
you're sick,

But here's what I
prescribe for you

COTTON

ALCOHOL

Mercurochrome

Please get well extra quick!

VITAMINS

ADHESIVE TAPE

The doctor's bag is the ultimate pick-me-up. Each item in it conceals a sentiment. Lift up the cotton, for example: "Hope things are pretty soft for you until you're feelin' good as new." Its contents have kept up with the march of science: The 1940 version carried ether instead of vitamins.

*1957*

*1928*

*1928*

Best Wishes ~ FROM THE OFFICE
Hurry up and get well!
We not only miss you
WE NEED YOU!

CHEER UP
It might be worse!

Pick-Me-Ups:
The Twenties
& Thirties

A CHEERFUL
NOTE TO A
sick friend

*1931*

WARM WISHES
for
Your Speedy
Recovery

*1929*

Happy Thoughts for
A LITTLE SHUT IN

Of course I know it's not much fun
This being sick and staying
Inside all day when all your friends
Are all outdoors and playing ~~
But just remember this one thing
That though you're sick today ~
One day real soon you'll be all well
And then YOU ~ too can play

*1929*

CONGRATULATIONS
On the Success of Your Operation
And here's hoping it won't be long now until
you'll be up and about ~ just feeling fine!

*1930*

PLEASE GET WELL
For My Sake
I worry so because you're ill
I'm getting scores of wrinkles ~
So do get well before my face
Looks quite like ~~~
RIP VAN WINKLE'S!

*1929*

Hello There ~ Little Shut In!
This comes to hope you'll soon be
feeling fine again

*1930*

Please Get Well!

*1934*

R/x-- Add lemon and soda water to taste. Stir well. Take as desired.

Just a little *"bottled moonshine"*
For a friend of mine who's sick
Here's hoping it's effective
So you'll get well double quick!

*1931*

CHEER UP

*1931*

*1935*

Feeling Better?
Gosh, I'm TICKLED!!

*1931*

GLAD YOU'RE UP AGAIN!

*1932*

SORRY YER SICK

I BRANG YA UP ME REMEDY IT'S PERFECK FER WHAT AILS YA!

SPINACH

*1939*

Pick-Me-Ups:
The Thirties

During Prohibition,
"bottled-moonshine," or
medicinal alcohol, was
legal, and sold over a
million gallons a year.

GLAD TO HEAR YOU'RE BETTER
Just got news you're
"on the mend"
And hasten now this word to send
To say 'twill be a happy day
When word comes round you're
"all O.K."

*1929*

LAID UP FOR REPAIRS, EH?
DO A GOOD JOB WHILE YOU'RE ABOUT IT

*1931*

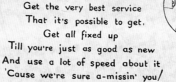

Have the old valves ground,
Have your carburetor set.
Get the very best service
That it's possible to get.
Get all fixed up
Till you're just as good as new
And use a lot of speed about it
'Cause we're sure a-missin' you!

So you've had a TONSILECTOMY!

You'll make some funny faces When you start to try to swallow...

Three topical get-well
cards from the forties.

*1942*

*1946*

*1942*

Pick-Me-Ups:
The Forties

CHEER UP!
This wish is like those
new LONG SKIRTS

(Dame Fashion's latest dish)--

1948

Hope You'll Soon Feel
Better!

WHEN I HEAR YOU ARE BETTER,
MY FACE WILL BE SO BRIGHT
THAT IF WE HAVE A BLACKOUT
THEY'LL HOLLER --

1943

Get Well Quick
NOW DON'T LET ANYBODY KNOW
WHAT THIS IS ALL ABOUT,
BECAUSE IT SURE WOULD BE TOO BAD
IF CERTAIN FOLKS FOUND OUT

THAT I'VE BEEN
HOARDING LATELY--
YES, IT'S ABSOLUTELY
TRUE--
THAT I'VE BEEN
HOARDING --

SUGAR    GASOLINE    SUGAR

1942

Sure was sorry when I heard
You'd been feeling "not so well"--

Hope it won't be long until
You'll be up and raising--

YOUR VICTORY
GARDEN

1942

PLEASE HURRY UP
AND GET WELL!

If GERMS must bite
As germs will do-

1940

TO SOMEONE WHO'S SICK ON
THANKSGIVING

'Sno fun being
sick at
a time such
as now

But this
brings you
along with

GOOD WISHES-

1943

SORRY YOU'RE SICK

JUST LIKE A PREFABRICATED HOUSE--

1947

1943

For Your "DU-RATION"
In Bed

This shortage
situation
Has got us all
perplexed

They've rationed
SUGAR, TIRES and GAS
And goodness knows
what next;

72

UP, AN' ATOM!

*1954*

You Sick?

HOPE YOU'LL SOON BE --

HURRY AND GET WELL...

Pick-Me-Ups:
The Fifties & Sixties

*1960*

NO TONSILS, HUH?

The Tonsils Out Club welcomes you--

You're IN without a doubt,

*1959*

CHEER UP! The cost of living's Gone SKY-HIGH,

GROCERY

CLOTHING STORE

*1958*

DO WHAT 4 OUT OF 5 DOCTORS Recommend

*1960*

A GET-WELL MESSAGE FROM ALL OF US

FLOWERS BOOKS

TO CHEER YOU UP, WE COULDA BOUGHT SOME FLOWERS OR A BOOK, BUT WE DID SOMETHIN' DIFFERENT--

*1959*

SORRY YOU'RE SICK

HERE'S SOMETHING TO HELP PASS THE TIME WHILE YOU ARE STAYING IN-- READ ALL ABOUT

CANASTA

*1950*

AN ILLNESS IS LIKE A TV COMMERCIAL--

*1965*

Kind of FLAT and OUT OF TUNE?

*1987*

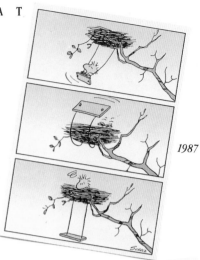

Just a little reminder after your operation -- Even the best constitution...

*1976*

*1987*

**Pick-Me-Ups:
The Sixties, Seventies
& Eighties**

GET·WELL·QUICK···

AND·DON'T·SPARE·THE·HORSES···

*1961*

*1962*

GARAGE

*1987*

each & every one of us wishes
you a speedy recovery.........

*1962*

74

# The Girls

"The American woman loves greeting cards," says a Hallmark man. "She likes to receive them, to send them, to shop for them." In fact, she sends about 90 percent of them—many to her bosom buddies. But the girls have always shared a lot; they've played Mah-Jongg and played dumb, they've poured at club meetings and sipped at Schrafft's, joined the feminists and the PTA, studied the mambo and the etiquette of smoking, rolled bandages and riveted, given each other home permanents, sold each other Tupperware, traded recipes from *The Joy of Cooking* and *The Joy of Sex,* watched for the male and watched for the mail.

*1956

*Happy Birthday…
from the girls!

1942

Nylons were scarce in
1942, but a girl still
had plenty to put on—
and take off.

*1931*

*1937*

*1935*

A Lot of Ladies:
The Twenties,
Thirties & Forties

*1922*

*1941*

*Lamour*
*you have*
*the better shape*
*you're in!*

*Happy Birthday!*

*1943*

*1941*

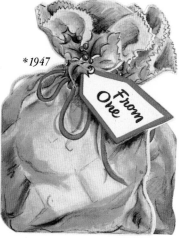

*From One...Old Bag to*
*Another. Merry Christmas*

*1947*

*1942*

No woman likes to admit her age, but here the secret's out of the closet. If birthdays were like clothes, they'd give you less to worry about every year; if they were like runs, maybe no one would notice them; if they were like slips, they'd come off leaving you in great shape.

1956

Pat Nixon didn't have a mink coat, but many a respectable wife of the fifties did. And—whether the mirror reflected a Fair Lady or a Red-Hot Mama—she also had a sense of humor about herself.

SEEMS LIKE OLD TIMES....

1958

IT'S LEAP YEAR, TIME, BUT WHO NEEDS MEN?!! !??!

1960

WHAT'S THE MATTER, COUNTESS ???

1956

1956

1956

...LOST THE COUNT ?

HAPPY BIRTHDAY!

DON'T WORRY DEAR!

1956

To a gal in her "EARLIES"-

*1956

*I would have sent you a mink...*

FROM ONE
FAIR LADY...

A Lot of Ladies:
The Fifties

*younger than springtime*

1958                1958

1957                *1956

1956                1959

1956

*Having a Birthday?*
*Well, don't be unnerved*
*We may not be young--*

*Of course I forgot your birthday--!*

*To a gal in her
"earlies"...
From one of the girlies!
Happy Birthday*

*Having a Birthday?
Well, don't be unnerved.
We may not be young...
But we're darned well-
preserved!!*

A Lot of Ladies:
The Sixties

The look. The girls got
younger and the skirts
shorter in the sixties.
Mod replaced mink,
and the role models
got more glamorous.
Jackie Kennedy was in
the White House,
Jacqueline Susann was
in the bookstores, and
Elizabeth Taylor was in
the news.

*Have FUN on your birthday! It's the SMART thing to do, Besides, at OUR age—*

1967

*JUST 'CAUSE WE'VE HAD SEVERAL, DOESN'T MEAN WE'RE ON THE SKIDS—*

1959                    1960

*interested in The NEW Cleopatra LOOK? JUST FoLLoW These SimPLE DiReCTions..*

1962                    1968

*ALL THE GIRLS ARE ANXIOUS TO KNOW—*

1960s

Happy Birthday
to someone who's
just turned 29

YOU'VE got
what it Takes to
wear a
CHEMISE...

*Why worry about BIRTHDAYS! We're still YOUNG and GAY—*

1968

Go, Girl, Go!

*1981   *STAND UP FOR YOUR
        RIGHTS AS A WOMAN!...LIE
        ABOUT YOUR AGE.

1987

A Lot of Ladies:
The Seventies &
Eighties

The girls today.

1988

1975

1988

Wanted to buy you one of those new STRING BIKINIS for your BIRTHDAY!

Another birthday and you've still got a great figure.

*I was going to send a
young sexy hunk over to
your house for your
Birthday...But then I
figured, why ruin his day.

*1988

FROM A POOR WORKING GIRL

I'M JUST A POOR WORKING GIRL, SLAVING AWAY,
BUT TAKING TIME OFF FROM THE
TOIL OF THE DAY

*1959*

A Valentine for You

If you don't think I'd rather send A nicer card—you're wrong, But I'm just a poor little working girl

*1942*

A Poor Working Girl is continually swamped

With a million and one things to do,

*1959*

*1961*

Christmas Greetings from a Pore Working Gal

This greeting ain't fancy But after all, Pal,

*1942*

Birthday Greetings from a Poor Working Girl

If you don't think I'd rather send A nicer card-- you're wrong,

*1952*

A POOR WORKING GIRL

IS CONTINUALLY SWAMPED
With a million and one
things to do,

*1956*

*1966*

HAPPY HALLOWEEN FROM A POOR WORKING GHOUL....

As early as 1910, Marie Dressler was singing "Heaven will protect the working girl." A lot she knew. The working girl has always been the very model of self-reliance...and self-pity.

Merry Christmas From a Poor Woiking Goil

*1947*

BIRTHDAY GREETINGS
FROM A POOR WORKING GIRL

I'm just a poor working girl slaving away

from one hard working gal...!!

*1957*

Merry Christmas... or, as we say in the trade,

*1962*

*1981*

Christmas Greetings from a POOR WORKING GAL

This greeting ain't fancy
But after all, Pal,

*1949*

FROM A POOR WORKING GIRL

I'm just a poor working girl slaving away But taking time off from the toil of the day To send you a wish that's the merriest kind—

*\*1956*

Merry Christmas
FROM A POOR
LITTLE WORKING GIRL

IT'S JUST A LITTLE CHRISTMAS CARD
I WISH THAT IT WAS MORE
BUT I'M JUST A PORE LITTLE WORKIN' GIRL

*1946*

HAPPY BIRTHDAY
from one
hardworking gal...

SOME ADVICE TO A WORKING GIRL WHO WOULD LIKE TO GET A MAN'S SALARY.

*I'm just a poor working girl, slaving away,
But taking time off from the toil of the day...
To send you a wish that's the merriest kind—
Now I'd better sign off and get back to the grind.

*\*1956*

*Some advice to a working girl who would like to get a man's salary...get married.

1927

1930

1928

1930

1931

Because You Are Engaged

May the days of your engagement
Be as bright as skies in June
And your future years together
A delightful ~ honeymoon

Wedding Congratulations

Congratulations for your Wedding

MOVED!

# Wedlock

"Like fingerprints," said George Bernard Shaw, "all marriages are different." Indeed. A wife is Myrna Loy, Lucille Ball, Gertrude Berg, or Mamie Eisenhower. A husband is Ozzie Nelson, George Burns, George F. Babbitt, or the Duke of Windsor. And if home isn't a castle, it's a thirties bungalow with bric-a-brac on the whatnot and Jack Benny on the radio...or a fifties split-level with picture window, backyard barbeque, TV, Scrabble board, and a two-tone station wagon in the driveway. She wears an apron, and he reads the paper, 'til death do them part.

1957

*Happy Valentine's Day*
TO MY HUSBAND

MY ESCORT, MY FRIEND, MY CONFIDANT,

MY ZIPPER-UPPER, MY HANDYMAN, MY TEAMMATE, MY LOVER--

Besides that, you're a pretty good husband!

*1981*

*1961*

In 1961 the little woman was content with good housekeeping; by 1981 her husband had been housebroken.

HUBBY -- EVERYONE --

THE MAID, COOK, GARDENER,

CHARWOMAN, SEAMSTRESS AND LAUNDRESS--

JOIN ME IN WISHING YOU A VERY HAPPY BIRTHDAY

WITH A BIG KISS FROM EACH OF US!

*1984*

*1959*

Before the seventies, her
husband was the man
behind the newspaper.
Today, his wife's the
lead story.

*SMACK*

*1987*

For My
Husband

Congratulations on Your THIRD
Wedding Anniversary

*If all those weary cynics
Who think marriage is the bunk
And say they 'don't believe in love
And all that sort of junk"*

*1946*

*1987*

Birthday Greetings to Someone I Love
MY HUSBAND

*1932*

Man and Wife:
The Thirties & Forties

1943

For the female in World War II, V-mail was handy. While her husband was overseas, she was overworked: For both of them, life was a battle.

1960

1960

## Man and Wife: The Fifties

It was OK to poke fun at married life in the fifties. After all, the sit-com couple set the standard.

1951

1958

1958

1956

this is for always and always, dear...

1959

1983

1987

1985

Man and Wife:
The Sixties, Seventies
& Eighties

1982

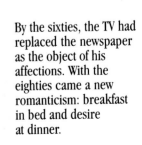

1977

1962

1987

By the sixties, the TV had
replaced the newspaper
as the object of his
affections. With the
eighties came a new
romanticism: breakfast
in bed and desire
at dinner.

# Dad

*H*e's been a Booster and a bugler, touting and tooting the American way. He's driven a flivver and a Thunderbird and tooted his own horn. He's pulled KP, but would never pull a Hoover at home. He's coached the Little League, lusted for Lana, mooned for Monroe, been undressed by Kinsey. He's read Spillane and Hemingway, scanned *Reader's Digest,* studied *Playboy;* cheered for DiMaggio, marveled at John Glenn, laughed at Gleason. He's coached the Little League, played by the rules, governed his family, and been put on a pedestal. And in greeting cards, he's been kept on it.

*1934*

Greetings TO FATHER!

Real Men:
The Twenties & Thirties

The 1924 card to a
bachelor—the oldest
card in this book—is
one of the few that
addresses a man's
unmarried state; one
never sees a card to
a widow or a spinster.

*c.* 1933

1933

1926

1933

1936

1924

*c.* 1931

1935

To THE "NEW FATHER" ON FATHER'S DAY

BABY CARE

THOUGH YOUR "PATERNAL ATTITUDE" MAY STILL BE PRETTY NEW,

*1949*

To My Pop on Father's Day

*1945*

Another Birthday?

That's all right, Old Man!

*1942*

A Valentine for POP

THE FINEST KIND OF VALENTINE IS ONE WITH LOVE IN EVERY LINE

AND WITH A MESSAGE, TOO, TO SAY,

"FOR SOMEONE SWELL IN EVERY WAY!"

*1944*

Christmas Greetings TO YOU IN THE NAVY

Three cheers for the Navy, And three cheers for you!

*1942*

*1944*

HI YA!

*1944*

*1945*

A Valentine FOR A SWELL BROTHER

IT'S BASES FULL AND BATTER UP AND NEITHER SIDE IS WINNING, IT'S THREE AND TWO WITH TWO AWAY AND IT'S THE FINAL INNING!

Real Men: The Forties

Happy Father's Day to Daddy

*1945*

### Real Men:
### The Fifties

The family moved to the suburbs and dad went outside. Post-war expansion was evident everywhere: in his house, in his waistline, in his wallet. In cards, there was also a new development: the photographic still life. It was ever so literal, but dad was hooked.

1958

An evergreen from the fifties…and a staple for dad. Mom gets hers, too.

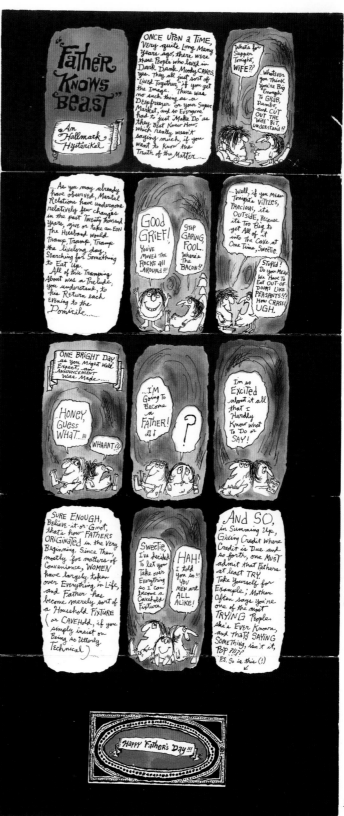

Weird humor, odd colors…An Hallmark Hysterikal for the Age of Aquarius.

*1962*

*DAD*, this brings more wishes
Than a hardware store has nails...

Than a
baseball game
has hot dogs,

And a
railroad line
has rails...

More wishes than the sea has fish

And a park has campers, too...

And every wish is guaranteed
To be filled with love for you!

HAPPY
VALENTINE'S DAY

*1987*

**Real Men: The Sixties,
Seventies & Eighties**

*DAD*, this isn't any Soft
SOAP...

*1970s*

*1963*

Happy Father's Day
to DAD--

The head of
the herd !

*1987*

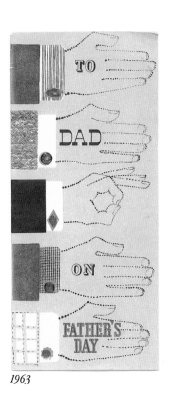

TO

DAD

ON

FATHER'S
DAY

*1963*

*1987*

FATHER

*1975*

FOR A
NICE
DADDY

Home is the hunter.
Once portrayed as
outdoorsman,
handyman, and
everything but a father,
dad is finally put in his
place—with the kids.

1936

1931

1981

1941

1987

1959

1943

1949

Dad's easy chair: his throne, his podium, his headquarters, his refuge. Pets and kids usurp it at their peril; mom decorates around it. Wake up, dear… it's bedtime.

1933

1949

1938

1944

1945

1987

1933

1938

1933

c. 1930

Dad's duds
and doodads

FOR YOU
on
FATHER'S DAY

*1931*

A
Happy Father's Day
to You

*1948*

*1930*

For
Dad

*1939*

Something to Help
Wish You a
Happy Father's Day

*1943*

For
Dad and

Mother
on
FATHER'S
DAY!

*1931*

SHORT
But never OLD —

*1932*

DAD'S BEST

PUT THIS IN
YOUR PIPE
AND
SMOKE IT!

Every day
is Father's
Day to me
because —

*1933*

I'LL BE BRIEF ABOUT
IT -- DAD —

JUST IN
CASE
YOU HAVE
FORGOTTEN —

*1931*

# Mom

In sunshine and shadow, wartime and peace, sickness and health, Mom's the word. With or without a chicken in every pot, she's kept the home fires burning. With true grit, she's hauled ice, scrubbed with Bon-Ami, tended Victory Gardens, saved peach pits, mastered the Waring blender, censured Ingrid Bergman, and gone for JFK. With gritted teeth, she's endured our music, our garb, our slang, and our friends. Sustained by Dr. Spock and Dr. Seuss, Aunt Jemima and Uncle Ben, she's shepherded her flock to suburbia and from it. She's stroked our egos and healed our wounds, tucked us in and dusted us off, dried our tears and tried our patience. She's been there to kiss us . . . and stayed there to miss us.

TO MOTHER'S APRON STRINGS

1928

Loving Thoughts on Mother's Day

1959

To My Wife on Mother's Day You're a wonderful Wife and Mother

FOR MOTHER'S DAY

To the MOTHER OF A FRIEND

1949

1933

1941

Mother country: her pots,
her pans, her province

A valentine for Mother

c. 1954

*1933*

*1931*

Mother Superior:
The Thirties

*1938*

*1933*

*1932*

*1934*

*opposite page:*
No mother gave more than a gold star mother, who lost a son in the war: "Though he has gone, you know he went/ With gallant heart and true, /A hero in his country's eyes, /A splendid son to you; / And all your memories of him/Will be a special part/Of that rich store of love and pride/That fills a mother's heart."

*1932*

*1931*

*1933*

THE YOUNGER GENERATION, MOM, COULD LEARN A LOT FROM YOU--

*1958*

A Mother's Day Greeting to You from Mother

*1949*

Thinking of You on Mother's Day

*1939*

Mother Superior:
The Forties & Fifties

To a Gold Star Mother

*1943*

ENJOY MOTHER'S DAY--

*1958*

'Cause school's out soon! HAPPY MOTHER'S DAY

*1958*

To you, MOTHER, on MOTHER'S DAY

Mothers are DOCTORS, SEAMSTRESSES, COOKS,
They're PREACHERS, and TEACHERS, and READERS of BOOKS,
JUDGES, and BANKERS, and WATCHERS of CLOCKS,
LAUNDRESSES, SCRUBWOMEN, MENDERS of SOCKS,
They're STARTERS and STOPPERS, and BAKERS of TARTS,
HEALERS of BRUISES and small BROKEN HEARTS,
HOUSEMAIDS, and GARDENERS --to them a ROSE

*1959*

To the Sweetest Mother in the Easter Parade

*1958*

To my HUSBAND'S MOTHER on Mother's Day

Because I think so much of you In such a special way,

*1941*

1962

IF IT WEREN'T FOR MOTHERS THERE WOULDN'T BE OTHERS

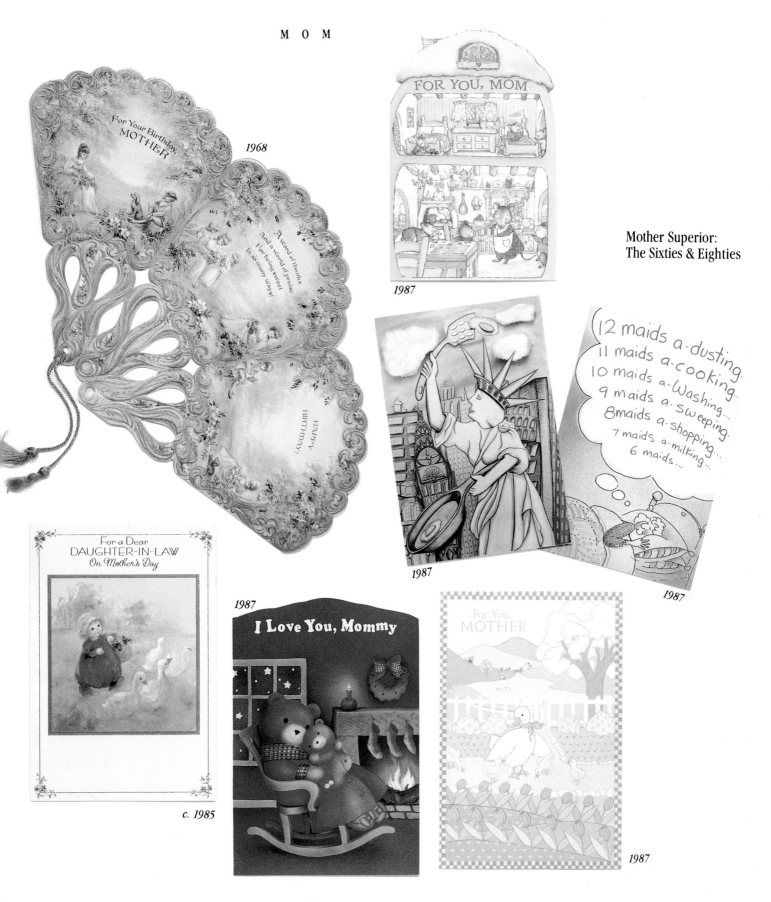

*For Your Birthday MOTHER*

*1968*

FOR YOU, MOM

*1987*

Mother Superior:
The Sixties & Eighties

12 maids a-dusting.
11 maids a-cooking.
10 maids a-Washing...
9 maids a-Sweeping.
8 maids a-shopping...
7 maids a-milking...
6 maids...

*1987*

*1987*

For a Dear
DAUGHTER-IN-LAW
*On Mother's Day*

*c. 1985*

*1987*

I Love You, Mommy

For You,
MOTHER

*1987*

To Son and His Wife
AT EASTER

*1960*

Happy Easter

*1960*

Pâques!

*1938*

## Garden Variety

he orchid and gardenia have gone the way of the wristlet and corsage. The geranium has thrived with the popularity of the patio. Spring brings the tulip, daffodil, and spray of dogwood blossoms; fall, the chrysanthemum, and Christmas, the poinsettia. But a rose is a rose is a rose is the pick of the crop, according to perfumers, florists, Kennedys, Lancasters, and the Hallmark computer. It is a symbol of love, friendship, beauty, perfection, inspiration, and victory—and a bloom for all seasons.

EASTER PEACE BE WITH YOU
May abiding faith show you the way
Of deep content on Easter Day
As comes to you the old sweet story
Of the risen Christ and Easter Glory

*1928*

On Your
EIGHTEENTH
Birthday

*1936*

To My Wife on Our Anniversary

*1960*

Thank You So Much

*1948*

With Our Love to Mother on Valentine's Day

*1949*

For Your Birthday, GRANDMOTHER

*1948*

To Let You Know I'm Thinking of You

Pansies stand for thoughts, says Hallmark's Jeanette Lee. They also grace the best-selling card of all time, the pansy basket at right.

*1939*

Best Wishes On Your Birthday

*1960*

TO MAMA On Mother's Day

*1939*

Glad Your Operation's Over

*1966*

*Valentine Greetings to my* OTHER MOTHER

*1928*

*Congratulations On Your Wedding*

*1943*

Happy Birthday

*1930*

*A Birthday Message for GRANDMOTHER*

*1938*

לְשָׁנָה טוֹבָה תִּכָּתֵב
HAPPY NEW YEAR, SWEETHEART

*1930*

Like the busiest bee or butterfly, the colorist's hand fluttered from petal to petal, decorating each card individually. Soon, though, cards were colored mechanically— and during World War II, they all seemed to be colored red, white, and blue.

*1938*

*A Birthday Message to My* SWEETHEART

*1928*

JES' SUPPOSIN'

Jes' supposin' you were here
Or I was there with you
And we could get together
As we often used to do
And talk awhile and laugh and smile
Without no pomp or posin'
Or frills or fuss~but just be us~
Doggone it!
Jes' supposin'!
Happy Easter

*A Gift for You With Our Best Wishes*

*1959*

The Rose

For You, Mother, from Your Daughter

*1956*

*1932*

A MOTHER'S DAY WISH For Mother

For Someone Nice On Sweetest Day

*1960s*

To the One I Love

"How Do I Love Thee?"

*1958*

For Someone Who Will Always Be Young

*1958*

To the Sweetest Mom in the World

*1952*

## Baby Faces

When the wind blows, the cradle will rock Not only did the Depression lower the price of pabulum, it also lowered the number of babies who consumed it—proving that blessed events seem to result from national ones. When we entered the war in the early forties, the birth rate increased a notch as our boys left pregnant brides behind them. When they came home, there ensued the Baby Boom: in 1945, we had 2.9 million babies, and in 1946, an astounding 3.4 million. The fifties were even more fruitful, what with push buttons and tail fins, suburban family rooms and...families; 1957 produced the highest birth rate (4.3 million) in U.S. history. The Baby Bust, from the early sixties to the mid-seventies, was probably due to the Pill and legalized abortion, but then came what the Census Bureau calls the Echo Effect. In 1986, Baby Boomers hatched 3.7 million of their own babies to be pampered and Pampered—the same number as born in 1948.

Some RATTLING GOOD NEWS

*1920s*

114

There's NEWS to report ——

*1942*

A New Arrival

*1947*

REAL PRESIDENTIAL TIMBER

*1925*

PRESENTING
(BY SPECIAL PERMISSION OF THE COPYRIGHT OWNERS)
THE REAL LIFE DRAMA
A BUNDLE FROM HEAVEN
*Featuring*
THE NEW BABY STAR

FIRST SHOWN AT _____
IN _____ HOSPITAL
ON _____
AT _____ O'CLOCK
A TWENTIETH CENTURY PRODUCTION
SPONSORED BY
_____

*1941*

STORK HEIR-LINES, LTD.
*Announce*

*The arrival of a new model*

*1941*

*Announcement*
Nowadays we're seeing double
And hearing double, too;
Cause it's a
DOUBLE FEATURE
For us the whole day through!

*942*

The Stork Club:
The Twenties
& Thirties

*Early 1930s*

JUST DROPPED IN!

Arrived _____ Weight _____
Signed _____

*Early 1930s*

Announcing
*the*
ARRIVAL OF—

Official
RATION BOOK

SERIAL
NUMBER

IDENTIFICATION

(Name of Person For Whom Book Is Issued)

(Home Address)

(Present Address)

| | SEX | WEIGHT | HEIGHT | EYES | HAIR |

DATE OF BIRTH

ISSUED BY (Signatures of Issuing Officials)

*1944*

I've Arrived

*1948*

| A | B | C | D | E | F |
|---|---|---|---|---|---|
| Good For A Visit To Baby At The Hospital | To Visit Baby And Family At Home | Admission To See Baby's First Smile | To See Baby's First Tooth | To Hear Baby's First Word | To Watch Baby's First Step |
| 1 | 2 | 3 | 4 | 5 | 6 |

| G | H | I | J | K | L |
|---|---|---|---|---|---|
| Entitling You To Baby's First Picture | Invitation To Attend Baby's Baptism | Invitation To Baby's First Birthday Party | Good For Each Succeeding Birthday Party | Invitation To Graduation Exercises | Invitation To The Wedding |
| 7 | 8 | 9 | 10 | 11 | 12 |

*1958*

STORK HEIR-LINES LTD. Announce

*1958*

I'm Here!

*1958*

THE $64,000,000,000,000 QUESTION HAS BEEN ANSWERED

*1958*

We've Adopted a Baby

*1958*

U. S. INDIVIDUAL INCOME TAX RETURN
FORM 1040

We've got a new

EXEMPTION...

ATTENTION!

"I pledge allegiance to the Flag . . . ."

*1943*

*1942*

HELLO
You know my Mom
and Daddy
And you know my Uncle Sam.

*1959*

Presenting A REAL LIFE DRAMA
JUNIOR MISS
Featuring A BRAND NEW STAR

FIRST APPEARANCE AT _____

ON _____ AT _____ O'CLOCK

A TWENTIETH CENTURY PRODUCTION

*1958*

*1958*

*1963*

*1981*

*c. 1960*

*1961*

*1960*

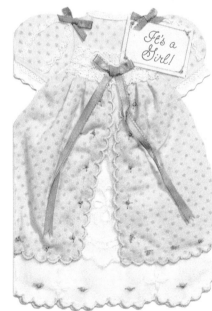

*1975*

The Stork Club: The
Forties through Eighties

*1971*

*1959*

117

Congratulations on the New Arrival

1942

And so "CONGRATULATIONS!"

And be sure to KEEP 'EM FLYING!

1958

To the New Parents.

Congratulations on your new "production."

1945

Two's company.

But three's---

1945

Birth Congratulations
Congratulations on the birth
Of just the sweetest
child on earth

1928

to the Parents of the
New Baby Boy

1950s

To Welcome Your
SECOND
BABY

1942

TWiNS!

WELL!

1934

Congratulations to the NEW PARENTS

There'll be quite a change in your "PROGRAM"
And the "BROADCASTS" will be
something new---

1944

Congratulations to the PARENTS

of the NEW PATRIOT

1942

**Rhapsody in Pink and Blue: The Twenties through Fifties**

*1981*

*1969*

*\* 1969*

*1968*          *1971*

*1958*          *1950s*

*Congratulations on Your Baby Girl*

SUGAR AND
SPICE?
HOW NICE!

*1968*

*\*Hear you have the "latest
model," The "smoothest" of
the year...So here's a little
"extra chrome" To
decorate the rear!*

*1981*

Rhapsody in Pink and
Blue: The Fifties
through Eighties

# Bon Voyage

orld War I put a moratorium on many pleasures, including travel abroad. When peace returned in 1919, so did the leisurely ocean voyage aboard the *Olympic*, the *Berengaria*, the *Aquitania*, the *Mauretania*. During the Depression, the well-heeled could sail around the world in eighty-five days for $749. After Lindbergh's soaring success came bumpy passenger planes. Then cars, highways, tourist courts, and Burma-Shave. In 1939, *everyone* could come to the Fair. Today, we go every which way: by foot or by Concorde, on a package tour or grand tour, with a backpack or Vuitton, down home or far from it.

1984

Wish you could tuck me in ~ your trunk and take me along!

BEST WISHES FOR A HAPPY TRIP

1929

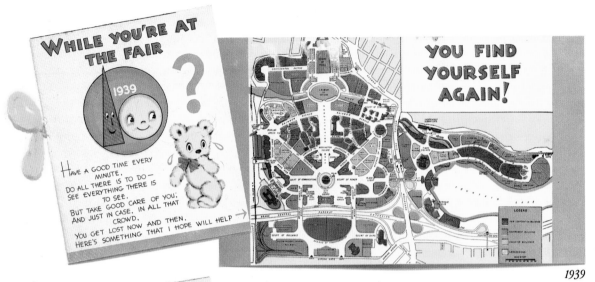

*1939*

While war clouds gathered over Europe, Americans flocked to the 1939 fairs in New York and San Francisco.

*1939*

*1939*

Signs of the times:
Burma Shave ads were a
road-side attraction (and
a welcome distraction)
in the thirties and
forties; by the fifties,
billboards were an
affliction.

*1987*

*1950*

*1980*

The family station wagon might be fine for some, but the sophisticated traveler seeks a more glamorous vehicle. In the fifties, it was a plane; today, the cruise ship is a hot ticket.

*1947*

*1932*

*1932*

A Fond Farewell:
The Thirties & Forties

It's *soigné* to say goodbye
in French, and Hallmark
indulged those who
couldn't: "*Bon Voyage!*
...Even if I can't
pronounce it!"

*1935*

*1948*

*1942*

*1929*

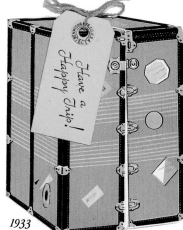

*1933*

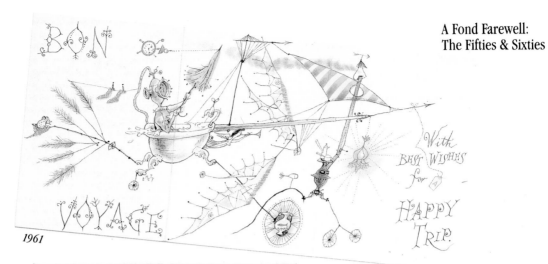

A Fond Farewell:
The Fifties & Sixties

*1961*

*c. 1957*

*   How about bringing me
    back a souvenir from your
    vacation?... Something
    about 6' 1" 170 lbs with
    dark curly hair, blue eyes,
    muscular, and loaded
    with money!

*1958*

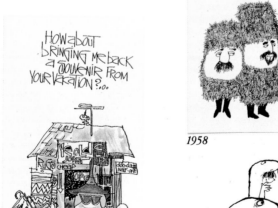

* *1958*

*Welcome Bach!*

*1962*

* *1962*

# Hard Times

hile Mae West swaggered and Fred swung Ginger, the Depression engulfed us. A pair of men's shoes cost $4 but who had $4? Who had work? The only good break came in 1933, when Prohibition was repealed. We've been up to our ears and down on our luck. We've endured bread lines and black lists, rations and inflations, recessions and strikes, Vietnam and Watergate, hot air and cold war. But even in the worst of times, when there have been no pennies from heaven and nobody's brother could spare a dime, we've been able to send a card.

*1932*

1932

1933

1932

1932

In spite of the occasional temperance card, for the most part Hallmark commiserated with those in need of spiritual revival.

## SEASON'S GREETINGS

Well, here it is [DEC 25] time for Christmas again. Doesn't seem possible, does it? [DREAM] --- Doesn't seem like a year has passed already Things haven't changed much Still have gangsters, --- still have graft --- STILL- have prohibition.

There's a great institution --prohibition. It's done the COUNTRY a lot of good. Take the corner druggist You take him. I don't want him. How would he feel with a saloon for a next door neighbor? How would you feel? How would I feel? How would ANYBODY feel??

Take our big BOOTLEGGERS. Look what they've done for the U.S. COUNTRY And what thanks do they get? The GOVERNMENT prosecutes them- puts 'em in jail At least it's rumored that the government put one of 'em in JAIL once--

That's prohibition - for you! For YOU -- not me No matter how you look at it -- It all gets back to the same thing. Take a JIGGER of GIN and some LEMON JUICE. Or maybe you'd better make it TWO JIGGERS. It's all right with me --
It's your stomach

And there YOU ARE! That is you, isn't it? And it's HOLIDAY TIME again -- FINE! -- Go ahead and have "A MERRY CHRISTMAS" They're not prohibited

## CHEERIO!

*1932*

128

1938

1932

1926

In flush times, economic hardship is an embarrassment to be concealed. During the Depression, it was a plight to be shared. Not even greeting cards could escape the reality of rumbling stomachs and tattered clothes.

1932

1935

1932

1942

GREETINGS!
you have been
drafted in the
WAR ON
POVERTY!

*1966*

*1958*

*1958*

In the aftermath of the
Depression, the
downswings of the
economy were called
recessions. The one in
1958 was quite serious,
with over five million
unemployed. A time-
honored cure for hard
times is wartime.

DO YOUR
BIT TO
CURE THE
RECESSION

*1958*

*1959*

CONGRATULATIONS!!!

*\* c. 1961*

*\*Congratulations!!!...rumor
has it that you've landed
a job with that rich uncle
of yours!!!!*

# Wartime

During World War I, Joyce Hall wrote in his autobiography, "We made cards that were tied with red, white, and blue ribbons and featured military symbols. But we soon found out that the men really wanted cards just like those sent at home." The second time around, Hallmark was a bit more aggressive, with plenty of pokes at the enemy—and this time the men could enjoy them. World War II launched a veritable attack on the post office. Mountains of magazines, sugar and sewing needles, love letters and V-mail crossed the seas—and brooked the censors. But greeting cards, with their effective images and very affective words, sailed through.

1944

As this card by Mort Walker suggests, wartime humor could be deprecating, but probably hewed close to the tedious and petty routine of a soldier's life.

1943

Greetings to You in the NAVY

1942

1942

1941

1940

1943

1942

WELCOME BACK

It's grand to have you
back again
And you can bet a million
It sure seems swell
to say to you
Well ––

HELLO THERE,
CIVILIAN!

1945

# Across the Miles

The football coach remembers his second-grade teacher, the suntanned retiree thinks of her frostbitten canasta club, the newlywed longs for the old folks at home. Friendship Day, created by Joyce Hall in 1919 and officially observed on the first Sunday of August, has probably never caught on as a major holiday because there's no need for it. True friendship is for keeps. And true friends, with or without Congressional sanction, keep in touch.

*1930*

Happy Easter Wishes for THE FOLKS AT HOME

There are friends we meet as we journey along
Who ~ like ships that pass in the night ~
We meet one day and they drift away ~
Silently ~ out of sight

There are other friends whom we chance to meet
Who prove loyal and staunch and true ~
Who tug at our hearts when the Yuletide starts
Just such a friend are YOU

1928

JUST SUCH A FRIEND ARE YOU

A FRIENDLY THOUGHT OF YOU

Give me everything that's modern
Up-to-now.... and nothing less....

give me radios and airplanes...
give me books...
right off the press

give me all the late
improvements...
give me everything that's
new
WAIT a minute!....
one exception....
give me...
OLD FRIENDS
just like you!

1934

How rapidly styles change. The hand-painted card of the twenties, with its satin ribbon, is elegant but somewhat generic; the card of the thirties, with its visual references, is aimed at a more stylish crowd.

*You're Just* THAT KIND of a FRIEND

*1931*

ACROSS
THE SEAS
AT
CHRISTMAS

*1938*

Keeping in Touch:
The Twenties & Thirties

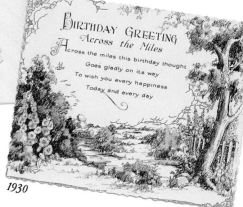

BIRTHDAY GREETING
*Across the Miles*
Across the miles this birthday thought
Goes gladly on its way
To wish you every happiness
Today and every day

*1930*

*Don't cha write*

*1933*

VALENTINE GREETINGS
*To the Folks at Home*

*c. 1933*

*1932*

*Christmas Greetings Across the Seas*

*Merry Christmas to the Home Folks*

*1936*

*c. 1928*

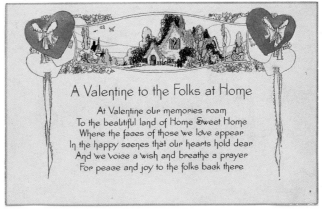

A Valentine to the Folks at Home

At Valentine our memories roam
To the beautiful land of Home Sweet Home
Where the faces of those we love appear
In the happy scenes that our hearts hold dear
And we voice a wish and breathe a prayer
For peace and joy to the folks back there

thinking...

*Across the Miles to You in the SERVICE*

*I SURE FEEL ANYTHING BUT SWELL WHEN WE'RE APART—GOOD NIGHT!*

WHEN SHERMAN SAID THAT WAR IS—

1943

THE UNITED STATES POST OFFICE

is a fine department of the Federal Government, whose TIRELESS WORKERS bring letters right to your door, through STORM, SLEET, and HAIL. They are trustworthy and loyal

1958

1955

You ought to be a FOREIGN CORRESPONDENT

1974

## Keeping in Touch: The Forties through Eighties

*Thinking of You.
    Now ADOLPH And BENITO
        And MISTER HIROHITO
    Are three geezers that I'd
        give up in a minute.
    But you bet your BOTTOM
        DOLLAR
    That I sure would raise a
        HOLLER
    If the world had no SWELL
        PEOPLE like YOU in it!*

THINKING OF YOU

Now Adolph and Benito And Mister Hirohito Are three geezers that I'll give up in a minute.

*1942

1961

ACROSS THE MILES at CHRISTMAS

ISSUED BY JUST-A-PEEK and OHIO RAILWAY COMPANY ROUND TRIP TICKET HERE THERE AND RETURN ALL THE COMFORTS OF HOME THE BEST WAY TO RIDE THE RAILS

I wish this Christmas greeting was a ticket for a train

1959

Across The Miles AT CHRISTMAS

Thinkin' of You

Here I am all by myself As lonesome as can be,

1943

Christmas Greetings ACROSS THE MILES

If wishes were HORSES Or AUTOS or PLANES Or ROLLER SKATES, BICYCLES, SCOOTERS or TRAINS, You bet that I'd be there In Person to say

1942

c. 1960

1935

1936

*Greetings from* CALIFORNIA

*This card is bathed in sunshine / Till it's turned a golden hue, / And it brings the warmest wishes*

America's favorite vacation and retirement spots in the thirties were California and Florida, and Hallmark could get away with the same picture and verse for both: "The sun is warm,/ The flowers are gay, /The birds sing sweet and clear—/ It would be Paradise today / If only you were here! Merry Christmas!"

1938

1935

Greetings FROM CALIFORNIA

Greetings FROM FLORIDA

1929

Christmas Greetings from OUT WEST
*This happy Christmas greeting, / The warmest and the best, / Brings the Best of Wishes, / From out the golden West / Merry Christmas*

Christmas Greetings FROM OUT WEST
*Out West a Christmas greeting / Is like a handclasp true / So an Out West / Christmas greeting / Is the kind I'm sending YOU*

1929

WELL HERE IT IS!
OPEN·IT
WHENEVER·YOU
DARN·PLEASE

1930

# Merry Christmas

Although they're praised for creating Thanksgiving, the Puritans heartily disapproved of Christmas. In 1659, a law was passed in Massachusetts fining any reveler five shillings. In New Amsterdam, however, the Dutch celebrated St. Nicholas's Day, and in Pennsylvania, the eighteenth-century Germans introduced Kriss Kringle and the Christmas tree to the New World. Out West, the trigger-happy rejoiced with turkey shoots, and down South with guns and firecrackers. By 1890, every state was making merry. St. Nick and Kriss Kringle had pretty much merged into Santa Claus, and Christmas had become the only religious holiday in America that is also a legal one. Now, as then, Yule logs are lit, halls are decked, trees are adorned, egg nog is nipped, carols are sung, stockings are hung, gifts are given, and greetings are sent. From Christmas, Florida, to Santa Claus, Indiana, from Mistletoe, Kentucky, to Holly, Colorado, over two billion cards are delivered every year.

Santa Claus:
The Twenties, Thirties
& Forties

To A Dear
Little Girl
Merry Christmas
the whole day through
May Santa Claus
be good to
you.

*c. 1930*

Merry Christmas,
GRANDDADDY

*1946*

Merry Christmas

*1936*

MERRY
CHRISTMAS
May Santa Claus
make you happy!

*1929*

*1941*

Season's
Greetings

*1931*

*1942*

We know this much
about him: Santa Claus
is fat and jolly; he has
a white beard and red
nose, a red suit edged
with white fur. Hallmark
found him this way in
the late twenties, and for
the next sixty years
didn't mess with the
basics…much.

"MERRY CHRISTMAS"
Easily read ~
Heartily meant
'Nuff said!

*1929*

With
BEST WISHES
for a
MERRY
CHRISTMAS

*1962*

Norman Rockwell
painted this Santa Claus
for Hallmark around
1950. Haddon
Sundblom's followed
about ten
years later.

*1952*

Santa Claus: The Fifties

*c. 1959*

*1954*

*1957*

*1959*

*1955*

*194*

*1955*

*1957*

*1957*

*For Some Nice Neighbors*

*1983*

*1985*

And what do **YOU** WANT FOR Christmas?

*1961*

*1968*

*1972*

*1987*

*1981*

Santa Claus:
The Sixties, Seventies
& Eighties

*1984*

1937

*Christmas Greetings TO THE BOSS*

With best wishes for happiness~
during the holiday season
and throughout the year
to come

1929

*Christmas Greetings to MY PLAYMATE*
To wish you lots and lots of happiness
on Christmas

1932

Dear Teacher,
A happy wish for
Christmas cheer~ And
for a glad and bright
New Year~ I've sent
this Card to you to
say~ Because I'm sure
you'd never guess~ What a
lot of happiness I wish
for you on Christmas Day

1929

*Merry Christmas, NURSE*

1929

*Christmas Greetings To the PASTOR*

A Christmas thought for someone
who is busy all the year
Doing good for other folks
and spreading joy and cheer
To hope that Christmas Day
and every day the whole year through
Will help repay you in a way
by being good to you

1930

1930

As early as the twenties,
Hallmark was catering
to the specific needs
of its customers. One
outstanding need seemed
to center on the boss.

*Christmas Greetings to THE BOSS*

To wish you Christmas
happiness
A day that's filled with cheer,
Good luck and real
prosperity
Throughout the coming
year

1930

*Christmas Greetings to THE DOCTOR*
It's easy enough to understand
The Christmas cheer throughout the land
It's because there are fine folks~
like you
To wish a 'Merry Christmas' to

1955, Dwight D. Eisenhower

1986, Ronald Reagan

1981, Ronald Reagan

1963

1977, Jimmy Carter

Four White House Christmas cards, and one angel painted by Jacqueline Kennedy to benefit the National Cultural Center.

Merry Christmas!
With Lots of Love for Daddy

*1929*

greetings

*1928*

SNOW plainer way of saying it ~
Merry Christmas

*1929*

Comfort and Joy:
The Twenties &
Thirties

Wish you a MERRY CHRISTMAS ?

*1932*

SEASON'S GREETINGS

*1928*

THERE'S NO MATCH FOR THIS ONE

*1932*

CHRISTMAS GREETINGS

*1928*

I sit by heck and scratch
my neck
And wonder what I'll send
you
Thoughts wander through
my muddled brain
From Buzz Wagon to
Candy Cane
But none of these quite
suit this year
So I'll just send a word of
cheer
A MERRY CHRISTMAS

*c. 1926*

JOYEUX NOËL ~
JOYEUX NOËL
Fifty million
Frenchmen can't be wrong!

*1929*

*1932*

*1928*

### Comfort and Joy: The Twenties & Thirties

Among these cards are some of Hallmark's most sumptuous offerings of the twenties.

*1929*

*1928*

*1931*

*1929*

*1928*

*1929*

*1929*

*1930*

It may be a little
ANTIQUE
but ~ ~
*It's Genuine!*
MERRY
CHRISTMAS

CHRISTMAS GREETINGS

HOOVER SAYS ECONOMIZE

AND SO I AM, YOU BET

HENCE ALL MY FRIENDS INSTEAD OF GIFTS

A CHRISTMAS CARD WILL GET

*1930*

Christmas Greetings
TO A GOLFER

Here's hoping all your putts will drop,
Your chip-shots stick like glue,
Here's hoping you will never top,
And always follow through,
Here's hoping all your drives are true,
With not one hook or slice
In other words here's wishing you
A GOLFER'S PARADISE

*1931*

Comfort and Joy:
The Thirties

*Merry Christmas*
Here's wishing you your
Favorite Brand
of cheer

*1932*

The whole darn family joins me

in wishing you

A MERRY CHRISTMAS

*1931*

For the man who was at
a loss to express himself,
there were macho
messages like that at
lower right: "Merry
Christmas…I really
don't go in so much /For
sentimental stuff and
such,/But still—its sort
of—you know—well,/
It's CHRISTMAS, fella—
what the __!"

*1931*

STILL
PERCOLATING
THE
SAME
GOOD WISHES

*1932*

*1939*

STATION "ME"
BROADCASTING

*1934*

*Merry Christmas*

*Merry Christmas*

*1941*

## Comfort and Joy: The Forties

The "soldier boy" in World War II was just that, a boy—far away from home, probably for the first time.

THOUGH YOU WON'T GET HOME THIS SEASON, STILL THERE ISN'T ANY REASON YOU CAN'T HAVE A "MERRY CHRISTMAS" WHILE IN CAMP, FOR ALL SOLDIER BOYS ARE BROTHERS AND JUST DOING THINGS FOR OTHERS IS A WAY TO KEEP YOUR SPIRITS FAR FROM DAMP.

NOW FOR CHRISTMAS CELEBRATIONS YOU MUST MAKE SOME PREPARATIONS AND THERE'LL BE SOME SPECIAL THINGS YOU'LL NEED, OF COURSE,

SO JUST GET A SPRIG OF MISTLETOE (YOU'LL BE SURPRISED WHERE THIS'LL GO) AND A PADDLE AND SOME ALUM AND A HORSE.

FOR THE SERGEANT WHO'S BEEN "NICE TO YOU" AND "SPOKEN ONCE OR TWICE" TO YOU, THERE OUGHTA BE SOME SPECIAL "PRESENT" DUE HIM,

SO YOU TELL HIM, "SHUT YOUR EYES, YOU! I'VE GOT SOMETHING TO SURPRISE YOU," WHEN HE SHUTS 'EM, BROTHER, GIVE THAT PADDLE TO HIM!

FOR THE BUGLER, WHO AT DAWNING STARTS YOU STRETCHING AND A-YAWNING, PUT THE ALUM IN THE MOUTHPIECE OF HIS HORN,

THOUGH WITH MUSIC HE'LL BE BRIMMIN' PUCKERED UP LIKE A PERSIMMON, HE WON'T PLAY NO REVEILLE ON CHRISTMAS MORN!

DON'T FORGET THE COOK, O NO SIR, JUST YOU TAKE THAT MISTLETOE, SIR, AND THEN HANG IT IN THE KITCHEN IN THE DARK,

TELL HIM SOMEONE WANTS TO MEET HIM AND WITH LOVING KISSES GREET HIM— WHEN HE "MUGS" THAT HORSE HE'LL THINK, "O WHAT A LARK!"

THIS SHOULD HELP YOU TO GET STARTED SO YOU WON'T BE TOO DOWNHEARTED 'CAUSE YOU CAN'T GET HOME TO VISIT FOR A WHILE, IF YOU'LL FOLLOW OUT THIS SCHEDULE WHEN THAT NIGHT YOU GO TO BED, YOU'LL HAVE SOME MEMORIES THAT OUGHTA MAKE YOU SMILE!

**MERRY CHRISTMAS AND HAPPY NEW YEAR!**

1940

1943

Santa's Helper

1953

## Comfort and Joy:
## The Forties

After the war, Andrew Wyeth's *Santa's Helper* appeared on a card, and so did Disney's Bambi, even if he wasn't on Santa's team.

1941

1941

1939

1948

1943

A CHRISTMAS PRAYER

*1950*

THE CHRISTMAS DANCE

*1951*

*1951*

*1950*

*1949*

SANTA'S SURPRISE

*1950*

*1951*

*1950*

Norman Rockwell painted about thirty Christmas pictures for Hallmark—the Dickensian scenes inspired by his childhood reading and the family situations which made him so popular.

1955

1950s

To My Darling
IN THE SERVICE
AT CHRISTMAS

1952

**Comfort and Joy:
The Fifties**

We decked the halls,
and Hallmark decked
the cards:
On Foil! On Glitter! On
Flocking! On Flitter!

Just a line ~~

1956

That "ENDS UP" in the usual fashion ~~

MERRY CHRISTMAS HAPPY NEW YEAR

1955

1956

Dashing through the Snow
In a one-horse open sleigh

*1950s*

*1955*

*1951*

*1955*

*1955*

*1962*

*1957*

*1957*

1952

"GOD BLESS US EVERY ONE"

c. 1950

1957

1953

Chartwell in Winter          Winston S. Churchill

*opposite page:*

*Christmas stars: Fred MacMurray, Lionel Barrymore, and Cecil Beaton painted these cards for Hallmark; Joyce Hall persuaded Winston Churchill to share his paintings as well.*

FOR YOU
AT CHRISTMAS

A pop-up card, reminiscent of the nineteenth-century mechanical.

*c. 1962*

1984

1972

1972

1984

Comfort and Joy:
The Sixties, Seventies
& Eighties

1972

c.1969

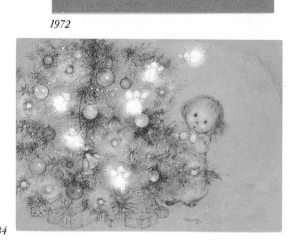

1984

1962

# *Acknowledgments*

*Little bluebirds have a mom to feed 'em worms and bugs. Little bunnies have a mom to give them bunny hugs...*I'm luckier. I had Sally Hopkins, manager collections and archives, Hallmark's indefatigable archivist, to feed me the goods, give me the resources, lead me through the halls, and put all her cards on the table....*And even little fish have moms to keep them off a hook. And little bookworms have a mom to help 'em find a book...*To help me find mine, I also had Bill Johnson, Hallmark's wry and incisive retired director of special projects; Jeannette Lee, retired vice president, corporate design; and Bob McCloskey, retired vice president, management/creative, Hallmark International, to contribute their reminiscences, observations, anecdotes, and wisdom; Don Dubowski, creative director, product discovery and development, to introduce me to Mary Hamilton, stylist, and Jim Smith and Art Carlson, master artists; Dean Walley, master writer, to show me his slides and teach me why some cards are only as good as their words; and an invaluable autobiography, *When You Care Enough,* by Joyce C. Hall with Curtiss Anderson....*Little kittens have a mom to wash their little faces. And little puppies have a mom to keep 'em in their places...* Wayne Wormsley, senior planner, season counter greeting cards, explained how the card lines are devised and put in *their* places, and Linda Monahan, product information system coordinator, reached into her computer to provide me with the awesome results of such planning....*Little bullfrogs have a mom to teach 'em how to croak. And little acorns have a mom to say they're oaky-doke...*As are Jon Henderson, manager creative resource center; Denise Johnson, editorial manager; Ann Wymore, product forecast analyst; Garry Glissmeyer, vice president, specialty creative and technical design; Diane Wall, marketing media relations manager; and Rosemary Dittmar-Cauthon, administrator at the Visitors' Center. They care enough to have shared generously. I am also grateful to two friends across the miles: Bill Cote, the editor of *Barr's Postcard News* in Lansing, Iowa, and Mary Dorman Lardie in Traverse City, Michigan, who, before her retirement from Hallmark in 1952, wrote volumes of verses—including the continuously popular *Little Bluebirds* borrowed here. My thanks, too, to Naomi Warner, Carol Rinzler, and Eric Himmel.

The author and publisher would like to thank everyone who granted the necessary permissions to reproduce cards, including the following:

Page 27, Minnie Mouse card © 1932 The Walt Disney Company; Page 28, Mickey and Minnie Mouse card © 1935 The Walt Disney Company; Page 30, Snoopy character © 1958 United Feature Syndicate, Inc. Used by permission of United Feature Syndicate, Inc.; Page 37, Mickey Mouse card © 1932 The Walt Disney Company; Page 45, Bulova card reproduced by courtesy of the Bulova Watch Company, Inc.; Page 45, Popeye and Olive Oyl characters © King Features; Page 45, Mickey Mouse card © 1935 The Walt Disney Company; Page 47, Donald Duck card © 1946 The Walt Disney Company; Page 57, Minnie Mouse card © 1985 The Walt Disney Company; Page 61, Mickey Mouse card © 1933 The Walt Disney Company; Page 62, Little Lulu character is a Trademark of/and © Western Publishing Company, Inc.; Page 70, Mickey Mouse card © 1934 The Walt Disney Company; Page 70, Popeye character © King Features; Page 74, Woodstock character © 1965 United Feature Syndicate, Inc. Used by permission of United Feature Syndicate, Inc.; Page 87, Dagwood and Blondie characters © King Features; Page 88, Fuller Brush card reproduced by courtesy of the Fuller Brush Company; Page 101, Father's Day Evening Post card used by permission of the Saturday Evening Post Company; Page 117, Peanuts characters © 1952, 1958 United Feature Syndicate, Inc. Used by permission of United Feature Syndicate, Inc.; Page 122, Burma Shave is a registered trademark of the American Safety Razor Company; Page 138, Bambi card © 1943 The Walt Disney Company; Page 152, Bambi card © 1948 The Walt Disney Company

Song lyric on page 6 from "'S Wonderful" by George and Ira Gershwin © 1927 WB Music Corp. (Renewed). All rights reserved. Used by permission

1933